WORK YOUR STRENGTHS

Work Your Strengths

A Scientific Process to Identify
Your Skills and Match Them
to the Best Career for You

CHUCK MARTIN

RICHARD GUARE, PH.D.

PEG DAWSON, ED.D.

AMACOM AMERICAN MANAGEMENT ASSOCIATION

New York · Atlanta · Brussels · Chicago · Mexico City · San Francisco
Shanghai · Tokyo · Toronto · Washington, D.C.

Bulk discounts available. For details visit:
www.amacombooks.org/go/specialsales
Or contact special sales:
Phone: 800-250-5308
E-mail: specialsls@amanet.org
View all the AMACOM titles at: www.amacombooks.org

This publication is designed to provide accurate and authoritative information in regard to the subject matter covered. It is sold with the understanding that the publisher is not engaged in rendering legal, accounting, or other professional service. If legal advice or other expert assistance is required, the services of a competent professional person should be sought.

Library of Congress Cataloging-in-Publication Data

Martin, Chuck, 1949-
Work your strengths : a scientific process to identify your skills and match them to the best career for you / Chuck Martin, Richard Guare, Peg Dawson.
    p. cm.
Includes index.
ISBN-13: 978-0-8144-1407-1
ISBN-10: 0-8144-1407-9
1. Vocational guidance. 2. Career development. I. Guare, Richard. II. Dawson, Peg. III. Title.
HF5381.M3714 2010
650.1—dc22

                                                                      2009049787

About AMA
American Management Association (www.amanet.org) is a world leader in talent development, advancing the skills of individuals to drive business success. Our mission is to support the goals of individuals and organizations through a complete range of products and services, including classroom and virtual seminars, webcasts, webinars, podcasts, conferences, corporate and government solutions, business books, and research. AMA's approach to improving performance combines experiential learning—learning through doing—with opportunities for ongoing professional growth at every step of one's career journey.

Printing number
10 9 8 7 6 5 4 3 2 1

To Agnes Martin and in memory of C. Leo Martin, my parents, for a lifetime of love, support, and encouragement.

CONTENTS

ACKNOWLEDGMENTS

There are many people we want to acknowledge and thank for their participation and help during the creation of this book.

We want to thank all of the business leaders, those executives and managers who took the time and effort to work with us on the study. They identified the high-performing people in their departments and organizations and forwarded them our questionnaire. In many cases, these managers monitored the completion of the questionnaires, collected them, and got them back to us for tabulation and analysis. Many of them also provided valuable feedback after being apprised of the results of the high performers in their organizations, for which we are grateful.

We also want to offer our appreciation to the members of NFI Research, the 2,000 senior executives and managers around the world who answer our bimonthly surveys and provide feedback and suggestions, as they have for the past decade. We want to especially thank all of those members who participated in the study as well as those who answered the surveys that appear in the book.

Thank you to Roger Kelleher at the American Management Association for inviting members to participate in the study and to Maryfran Johnson, editor in chief, *CIO* magazine and Events, for inviting *CIO* magazine subscribers to participate. And thanks to Carolyn A. Johnson, CIO research manager, for working with us to contact those IT professionals and for tracking the results with us.

To conduct such a project took a substantial team of researchers, all of whom we would like to especially thank. A special thank-you to the research team coordinators—Danielle Crepeau, Amy Prushinski, Andrew

Hatch, and Kathryn Rohlicek—who worked on the early stages of the project to identify categories and industries and coordinated with the researchers to organize, distribute, and collect the questionnaires and provide information back to the participants.

We are deeply grateful to the research team, who worked diligently to conduct the study in companies throughout the United States. So thank you Morgan Dorval, Phillip Hannafin, Brittany Hughes, Ashley Kelloway, Lisa Kemp, Joseph Madden, Melissa Nelson, Ryan O'Hara, Craig Parsons, Cali Rodriguez, and Lindsay Thibeault.

Thank you to the researchers from the Whittemore School of Business and Economics at the University of New Hampshire who helped in various stages of the research, some by contacting organizations to participate and following through to the questionnaire completions. So thanks to Anthony Azarian, Allison Bickford, Anthony Terlizzi, Courtney Sweeney, Casey Cardinal, Christina Rolli, Carling Belden, Christian Kramar, Christopher Croteau, Erin Badger, Fern Strasser, Gregory Halama, Jaclyn Moran, Jenna Vadala, Jessica Dusenberry, Kellen Millard, Kyle Rochefort, Kathleen Burns, Lauren McHugh, Mark Lanciani, Michael DeRoche, Nicholas Filias, Paige Pendleton, Patrick Hussey, Ryan Mill, Stephanie Mitchell, Theodore Bahtsevanos, Victoria Gellatly, and Zachary Lash.

Also thanks to researchers Allyson Gibbs, Aliza Aylward, Ashley Seely, Ariane Harter, Bryan Bartlett, Brenna Tenore, Brendon Sprinkle, Christine Frazier, Corey Marceau, Domenic Botticelli, Danielle Neuffer, Daniel Grube, Garrett White, Garrett Cypher, Jonathan Hinds, Jenna Cardarelli, Kayla Vigneault, Kristin Kendall, Kristen Schwaegerle, Keri Deming, Lauren Gordon, Lindsey Giovinelli, Michelle Sheehan, Nina Shaw, Patrick Poulin, Peter Stanieich, Steven Zimmerman, Timothy Brannelly, and Tyler Loopley.

Thank you to Christina Parisi, my editor at AMACOM, for insight as well as patience throughout the editing process, and to Jacquie Flynn, my original editor, now a literary agent at Joelle Delbourgo Associates, for having the foresight to grasp the concepts here.

Thanks to Aaron A. Reid, Ph.D., chief behavioral scientist, and his team at Sentient Decision Science, LLC, for insight and working with us on the reliability aspects of our survey.

A very special thank-you to the NFI research directors of marketing and publicity: Katy Peters, for creating the original data structure to be able to report on the study, and Cara Sandberg, for tracking and marketing the study results. And thank you to our directors of research, Kevin Wood-Friend, for creating the underlying technology that facilitated the data collection and analysis, and Daniel Lundquist, for conducting our bimonthly surveys as well as the study.

This book could not have been done without the unwavering support from my family, for which I am forever grateful. So my heartfelt and deepest thank-you to Teri, my loving wife and lifelong partner, and Ryan and Chase, our sons, for your constant encouragement and understanding and for always being there for me.

WORK YOUR STRENGTHS

Introduction

Finding the Right Job

YOU MAY BE a smart person but still feel you're in the wrong position at work or even the wrong career. And you may be right. Your brain is *hardwired* to function a specific way. If you're not in a position where your strongest skills are vital, you're not likely to excel. Worse, if you're in a position where your weakest skills are vital, you're going to feel it and are likely to fail. You won't look forward to going to work because what you do doesn't fit how your brain is wired. Your job will be unnatural and highly challenging. While the idea of finding the job most suited to you seems simple enough, there are many instances when it doesn't happen. Someone may convince you that you're the right person for a particular job or promotion, you accept it, and over time it doesn't work out as planned. Or you may get promoted because you've performed well in your current position, only to find out you're not suited for the new role. When this happens, nobody wins.

Over the course of a career, you may move from job to job until you finally fall into a position that seems perfect. It could be that over a long period of time you and many others end up in the right position, but it's often by chance.

But what if you could predetermine which position or career is the right one for you to increase your probability of success? Imagine if, as an individual, you could take years away from trial and error in jobs along your career path by scientifically determining in advance how well a particular position would suit you.

The purpose of this book is to provide you with that insight. It's the result of a two-year study we conducted to answer these and other questions. We sought to map certain cognitive skills of high-performing individuals to what they do and where they work. These skills are called *Executive Skills* because they help you execute tasks. The idea is to navigate yourself into positions that play to your innate strengths. It's about matching how your brain is wired to the job or task based on how the brains of those already successful in those jobs are wired. Though this isn't always possible from a practical standpoint in business, you'd still know when a certain task or function you're required to perform would be a good or a bad fit for your strengths and weaknesses and plan accordingly. You'd know in advance what kind of help you need to enlist.

Similarly, if you have people reporting to you or people you mentor, you could help them determine what role or job would be best for them. The best way to motivate is to get the most appropriate people in the positions most suitable to them. This is like the concept, familiar to many in business, of getting the right people in the right seat on the right bus.[1] We call this placing of a person in the correct job or position by matching Executive Skills with those required for the job *first-time right-seating.*

As an executive or a manager, imagine being able to promote and move subordinates along their career path knowing their inherent Executive Skills strengths and weaknesses. This knowledge could be helpful to determine where an employee is most likely to succeed. And if a certain position requires a person's weaknesses in one job along a career path, at least you'll know in advance so that appropriate support can be provided while the person is in that role.

Playing to Strengths Leads to Goodness of Fit

If you've held several positions in your career, you may recall that one was either a lot easier or a lot harder than others. This could have been an Executive Skills match or mismatch, where your strengths were those that were required for the job—or not.

When your strengths match those required for a task, it's called a *goodness-of-fit* situation. The main objective in understanding and utilizing Executive Skills profiling is to strive for positions that cause goodness-of-fit situations. This can help explain why a person isn't successful in one position and then changes positions or companies and becomes successful. While it may appear to observers that the person changed and improved, the reality is that the situation changed and better suited the person's Executive Skills strengths.

And when your strengths match what you do, you're more likely to be successful and even look forward to work because what you're doing there feels natural. This can lead to rewards, including compensation, bonuses, and promotions. As a successful person—a high performer—you will likely stand out among your peers and generally be acknowledged by management. And consistently using this knowledge can help you throughout your entire career.

If you're a manager, this knowledge can also make you a star, because you'll consistently place the right people in the right positions and can bask in the halo effects of their success.

More than 100 researchers worked on various parts of this study to help identify the cognitive characteristics of high-performing people in business.[2] We questioned more than 2,500 people at hundreds of organizations of all types, from Fortune 500 companies to nonprofits at every level, from employee to CEO. The goal was to provide you with a solid scientific method for finding your ideal field, job, and position.

Matching Strengths of High-Performing Individuals

The basis of determining a person's strengths and weaknesses in Executive Skills is well grounded in neuropsychology and revolves around those fixed functions associated with the frontal lobes. For many years, psychologists have used knowledge of the development of these functions from childhood through adolescence to provide guidelines for assessment and to help children and teenagers. However, it's only recently that this knowledge has been taken to the next level (notably in our last book, *SMARTS: Are We Hardwired for Success?*), which is helping adults like you use knowledge about these fixed skills for work and life.

This book attempts to advance this even further, by highlighting which specific Executive Skills are mostly found in the stars at work, those successful in business across a range of categories. There are specific similarities and differences by a range of categories of high-performing individuals:

- Employees, managers, and executives have different strengths, but they all share a common weakness.

- The most commonly found strength in high-performing males and females is different.

- Almost all high performers in information technology (IT) are not weak in one particular Executive Skill.

- IT executives are better at handling stress than IT employees.

- High performers who work in clinical departments are strong in one Executive Skill that is a dominant weakness of those in IT.

- High performers in finance, administrative, and sales share a common strength.

- CEOs and CFOs share the same three most commonly found strengths.

- High performers in marketing/advertising/promotion departments are not weak in a certain skill.

- There is one particular strength in high performers in customer service departments, and the overwhelming majority of high performers in customer service are not weak in it.

- There is one strength found in sales managers and executives that is not frequently found in sales employees.

- Of all high performers strong in one Executive Skill, 35 percent are either a CEO or CFO.

The Executive Skills

Our survey instrument for the study[3] enables you to clearly and easily identify your strongest and weakest Executive Skills, which we detail later. Knowledge of these functions enables you to play to your strengths while minimizing issues caused by the weaknesses. Your strongest Executive Skills will continue to be your strongest and your weakest will continue to be your weakest, because they're not dramatically changeable by the time you reach adulthood, which we detail later.

Although researchers have various ways of labeling, defining, and organizing Executive Skills, our model encompasses 12 separate skills that are most relevant to the way people function in a work environment.

Despite the term *Executive Skills*, whose use in neuropsychology dates back decades, there's no connection to executives at work and no connection to the traditional meaning of skills. Executive Skills should not be confused with functions or skills of executives, because Executive Skills are how the frontal lobes and associated brain areas manage information and behavior. And these are not skills that can be learned; they are cognitive functions that are hardwired into the brain from birth.

Each person has a set of strongest and weakest of these cognitive functions in their makeup. Generally, they have two or three that are their strongest and two or three that are their weakest. Those in the middle are not likely to get you in trouble, though they can't be dramatically improved either. Throughout the book, we focus on the three strongest and the three weakest of the Executive Skills across all high performers.

Everyone has this personal combination of strengths and weaknesses, and the mix varies from person to person.

There are 12 Executive Skills, and certain ones are prevalent in high-performing individuals in business.

1. *Response Inhibition:* This is the ability to think before you act. It is the ability to resist the urge to say or do something to allow time to evaluate the situation and how a behavior might affect it.

2. *Working Memory:* This is the ability to hold information in memory while performing complex tasks. It involves drawing on past

learning or experience to apply to the situation at hand or to project into the future.

3. *Emotional Control:* This is the ability to manage emotions in order to achieve goals, complete tasks, or control and direct behavior.

4. *Sustained Attention:* This is the capacity to maintain attention to a situation or task in spite of distractibility, fatigue, or boredom.

5. *Task Initiation:* This is the ability to begin projects or tasks without undue procrastination.

6. *Planning/Prioritization:* This is the capacity to develop a road map to arrive at a destination or goal, and knowing which are the most important signposts along the way.

7. *Organization:* This is the ability to arrange or place according to a system.

8. *Time Management:* This is the capacity to estimate how much time one has, to allocate it effectively, and to stay within time limits and deadlines. It involves a sense that time is important.

9. *Goal-Directed Persistence:* This is the capacity to have a goal, follow through to the completion of the goal, and not be put off or distracted by competing interests along the way.

10. *Flexibility:* This is the ability to revise plans in the face of obstacles, setbacks, new information, or mistakes. It relates to adaptability to changing conditions.

11. *Metacognition:* This is the capacity to stand back and take a bird's-eye view of yourself in a situation and to be able to understand and make changes in the ways that you solve problems.

12. *Stress Tolerance:* This is the ability to thrive in stressful situations and to cope with uncertainty, change, and performance demands.

You may go to www.workyourstrengths.net/profile to take the Executive Skills Profile one time at no charge.

Frontal Lobes and Executive Skills

The brain is a complex organ, and both neuropsychologists and writers for the popular press have attempted to paint a simplified picture to help people understand how it works and what part of the brain performs what function. Books have been written about left-brain and right-brain functions, with *language* being the skill most commonly attributed to the left brain, and *emotions* and *spatial concepts* being attributed to the right brain. In fact, it is more complex than that (the tone of voice with which someone speaks is interpreted by the right hemisphere of the brain, while the words are interpreted by the left hemisphere).

More broadly, there are portions of the brain responsible for perception, memory, language, and movement. But for an individual *to do* anything with all that information requires the activation of the frontal lobes. The frontal lobes of the brain—the portion of the brain just behind the forehead—are responsible for reasoning and decision making. In terms of brain functioning, the frontal lobes—and particularly the prefrontal cortex—are almost unique in their ability to receive signals from all other brain regions, thus enabling them to factor in previous experiences and prior knowledge, current biological states, and incoming information from the external world. It is for this reason that the frontal lobes are sometimes called the *central executive*. And Executive Skills are the mechanisms by which humans sift through massive amounts of information in order to reason and make decisions.

While specific skills associated with the frontal lobes have long been described in scientific literature, the usage of the terms *Executive Functions* or *Executive Skills* is more recent, dating back to the 1980s. However, in spite of their relatively young age, the terms are now commonly recognized in the neuroscientific literature and associated with frontal lobe activity. We detail more of the science behind Executive Skills and the brain in a later chapter.

The Spread Between Strengths and Weaknesses: The Differentiator

While we identified all 12 Executive Skills in high performers, we focus on the three highest and three lowest because those are the most likely either to provide the greatest help or to impede success. When a large percentage of high-performing individuals are strong in a certain Executive Skill, a corresponding large number are typically not weak in that same skill. In any given function or title, generally a third or more of the high performers with those titles or functions share at least one strength. When analyzing specific levels within a job function (such as sales executive), up to half of high performers share the same strength.

By area, such as a department, a significant number of high performers with the same title are not weak in one or two skills. Whatever the weakness a significant number of high performers did not have was also one of the top strengths in that particular group. We call this Executive Skill *the Differentiator,* and we identify it in each case throughout the book. It's this spread between strengths and weaknesses in high performers that determines the importance of a particular Executive Skill in any given area.

We have written this book both for you, for personal career planning, and for managers and executives, to help them more precisely determine who might be best suited for a particular position or job.

Executive Skills strengths and weaknesses cut across all industries, professions, and titles, because they're hardwired into a person's brain. The book is organized to give you a basis in understanding these skills and the details of the study, and ways to see which industries, departments, and jobs have high performers with the same strengths as you.

The ultimate result of our research is that we determined which Executive Skills reside in high performers at all levels across organizations. Executive Functions of many high performers at lower levels are different from those at higher levels in the same areas of work. This information, about which brains are in the best seats, is aimed at helping you and business leaders avoid the costly and disruptive step of the wrong person ending up in the wrong job. The goal of this book is to greatly increase the probability of finding the round peg for the round hole.

1

Determining Your Own Strengths and Weaknesses

. . . and Finding the Strengths and Weaknesses of Others

A FREQUENT QUESTION regarding the 12 Executive Skills is, Which skills matter most and which matter least? There's really no set answer because, as they say in psychology, it depends. If you're a high performer, different Executive Skills strengths and weaknesses are found in different situations or categories. While all 12 Executive Skills are found in all people, including high performers, only your strongest and few weakest matter most to you and are likely to impact your performance in any given situation.

Among high-performing individuals in various business departments and functions, there are common strengths and weaknesses, as well as typical combinations of Executive Skills strengths and weaknesses. Even without knowing about Executive Skills strengths and weaknesses, many successful businesspeople have intuitively figured out some of their own Executive Skills issues over a period of time. For example, if you're a high performer weak in Time Management, you may have concluded long ago that you needed someone to keep you on schedule and hired an executive assistant who does just that.

You may not recognize some of the other Executive Skills as easily, so understanding the characteristics and behaviors associated with all 12 can prove helpful. While each high performer will likely be strong in two or three skills and weak in two or three, knowing about all 12 can be helpful in interacting with other people, who may have a different Executive Skills profile.

Certain strengths and weaknesses are found in more high performers overall. However, each Executive Skills strength can be found in a particular job type, title, department, or industry, so if you're strong in one skill that's not found in high performers in, say, sales, it could be a strength of high performers in customer service, which we detail later. The point is that just because your strengths don't match those of high performers overall, there's still hope because they likely match a specific area, such as by a certain department or title. In some cases, there are a few high performers in positions where their strengths are not the same as the commonly found strengths in high performers in those roles. It's likely that these people are having a more difficult time because some of the tasks could feel unnatural to them.

Everyone has strengths and weaknesses in their skills. It would be extremely unusual for a person to be strong in all 12 skills because some are effectively opposites. For example, high performers weak in Time Management are also typically weak in Task Initiation, but they are strong in Metacognition, Flexibility, or Goal-Directed Persistence. And those strong in Time Management are low in Emotional Control or Stress Tolerance.

There are some common combinations of strengths and weaknesses, so people strong in specific skills often are weak in certain others.

Determining your strongest and weakest skill requires that you understand each of the skills and the characteristics associated with them. Several of the Executive Skills in which you excel or fail will be obvious to you right away. For example, you probably already know whether you're good at starting projects easily without procrastinating. Or you might feel that you're generally flexible or not. Just knowing that tells you that you are either strong or weak in that particular Executive Skill.

However, the key is to understand all 12 Executive Skills in relation to each other and learn the strength and weakness characteristics of each.

People typically have two or three strengths and two or three weaknesses, with the remaining Executive Skills falling somewhere in between. Those that are in between are not generally likely to get you in trouble, but those at the extremes can help you position yourself for greater successes and fewer failures. Those that are strongest will allow you to determine what tasks, projects, relationships, and even careers you'd find yourself comfortably matched to. Those that are weakest can show you personal situations and even jobs and careers that you should probably avoid. By matching your strengths to those of high performers with the same strengths, you may identify a job, a function, or even an industry where you might be a perfect fit. You also may find that you are a match for the job you already have, with Executive Skills that match those who are high performers in a similar job.

If you're an executive or a manager, once you know what behaviors typically go with each skill, then you can identify those behaviors in those who work for you and likely determine their strengths and weaknesses. Knowing your subordinates' strengths and weaknesses can help you interact with them more effectively and determine which roles or functions at work would better suit each person.

Following are the Executive Skills with the associated traits and behaviors that typically go along with them, as both strengths and weaknesses. Each skill was found as either a strength or weakness in between 40 to slightly over 60 percent of high performers overall. However, as you'll see later in the book, the significance of specific Executive Skills in high performers comes into play when viewed by job function, department, or industry.

Skill 1: Response Inhibition

This Executive Skill is about having the capacity to think before speaking or acting. Often it is what someone says that causes you to want to respond. It might be a discussion where your spouse casually mentions a person who's not in the room, and you quickly blurt out that she's a real jerk, within earshot of others who are her friends. Or it may be your boss, who takes his golf seriously, mentioning how well he did in his game over the weekend, and you immediately say you think golf is such a waste of time.

If you lean to informed decision making, generally take a methodical and deliberate approach to things, and are not often impulsive, you're probably strong in Response Inhibition. You also could easily suppress a response until you've thought about it.

On the other hand, if you often act on impulse, tend to say the first thing that pops into your mind, and generally act before you consider the consequences, you're probably weak in this skill. If you can easily remember a few things you said that you later regretted, that is a clue that Response Inhibition is not one of your strongest Executive Skills. Another clue is if you often feel like you want to kick yourself for what you just said. If you often want to kick others for what *they* just said, they're probably weak in Response Inhibition.

Another way to determine whether this skill is high or low for you is to recall how you've acted in past situations to determine whether you actually use this skill. For example, you'd be using this skill if you've worked around the clock finishing a project for a demanding client who then says he's not happy with your work and you answer him without losing your temper. Or when your boss suggests a bold, new initiative that looks good on the surface, you suggest assembling a meeting to discuss the pros and cons of doing it.

Skill 2: Working Memory

It's as if your memory is always *on,* no matter how busy you are or what you're doing. Working Memory involves the ability to hold information in memory while performing complex tasks. This is more than just recalling something from the past. It involves drawing on past learning or experience to apply to the situation at hand or to project into the future. If you never use a list to go shopping and always get what you need, you're probably high in Working Memory.

When you remember that you promised to get to your son's baseball game at 3 P.M. in the midst of an emergency that pops up at the office at 1 P.M., you're using the skill of Working Memory. If you're usually able to do one task and not lose sight of other commitments, you're probably strong in Working Memory. You'd also be considered to be reliable, counted on to follow through, and able to keep your eye on the ball.

You'd be using this skill when you remember to return an expense report your assistant asked for when you're working on a tight budget deadline. Or you remember you have a dentist appointment when you call the service station to fix your unexpected flat tire.

Conversely, if you're sometimes absentminded and need frequent reminders to complete tasks, you're probably weak in Working Memory. You'd likely miss an appointment because you didn't write it down, or you might leave your cell phone on your airplane seat because you were worried about making a tight connection. You might also have forgotten that a week ago you promised to meet your spouse for lunch today because something pressing came up at work late this morning. You really meant to, but you just totally forgot.

Skill 3: Emotional Control

This is the ability to manage emotions in order to achieve goals, complete tasks, or control and direct behavior. If you can keep your emotions in check to the point that they don't get in the way of what you're trying to do, you're probably high in Emotional Control. This skill involves making positive statements to yourself, suppressing negative self-statements, and even delaying immediate gratification while you pursue more important long-term goals.

If you're high in Emotional Control, you would not be easily sidetracked, would tend to get the job done, would be unemotional and cool under pressure, would be able to resist temptations that might lead you astray, would not easily be discouraged, and would be resilient in the face of setbacks. If you're strong in Emotional Control, you'd tend to find something positive in a negative performance review, be able to bounce back after an emotional upset, and be able to psych yourself up to make a phone call you dread.

If you're low in Emotional Control, you can be overly emotional and sensitive to criticism. You might go into a situation expecting to fail, tell yourself this is the worst presentation you've ever done, or find yourself dwelling all day on criticism you received in the morning. A common sign of low Emotional Control is having difficulty controlling anger, irritability, and frustration.

Skill 4: Sustained Attention

Sustained Attention is about having the ability to stick with something. It's the capacity to maintain attention to a situation or task. If you're high in Sustained Attention, you find it easy to stay on the task at hand, become immersed in that task, and screen out distractions. Even though you're tired at the end of the day, you'd rather complete the report you're writing because you know it will be easier to finish it now instead of beginning again the next day. You have a reputation for making deadlines because you can stick with things. Sustained Attention is having the capacity to maintain attention to a situation or task in spite of distractions, fatigue, or boredom. It's all about the ability to stay focused.

If you're weak in Sustained Attention, you have difficulty seeing things through to the end and can be easily distracted. People weak in Sustained Attention might have a performance review due in less than an hour but decide to check e-mail first. Or they might take work home to do over the weekend but save it for Sunday night, when they get sidetracked by a baseball game on television.

Skill 5: Task Initiation

If you tend to do something today rather than put it off until tomorrow, you're probably strong in Task Initiation, which is the ability to begin tasks or projects without procrastinating. Getting started on something would come easy for you, with an action orientation and propensity to get the job going without undue delay, in an efficient or timely fashion. You would tend to pay your bills as soon as you receive them and immediately tackle that project that is due in four weeks. You begin a task when you promised you would and generally hit the ground running as soon as you get to work.

If you're low in the skill of Task Initiation, you probably tend to procrastinate and are slow getting started on projects. You might seek that extra cup of coffee before getting down to work. You would also frequently (and with good intentions) prefer to start something tomorrow rather than today. There would always be something more interesting to do rather than start that project. Many high performers are weak in Task Initiation, especially at higher ranks in an organization.

Skill 6: Planning/Prioritization

This is the ability to create a road map to reach a goal. If you're strong in this Executive Skill, you can sequence priorities well and are efficient and clear-thinking. You probably make a list of steps required to complete a project and easily say no to a colleague's request for help if it means you can't finish your own project that's on a tight deadline. You're also able to decide between two courses of action based on the potential benefits of each. Planning/Prioritization involves being able to make decisions about what's important to focus on and what's not. It is the ability to identify and organize the steps needed to carry out your intentions or achieve a goal.

If you're low in this skill, you might not be sure where to start and be unsure of what's important, and can't seem to make plans. You tend to drop a well-thought-out project because a great new idea just presented itself or you have so much to do you can't decide what you should do next. Everything seems important, so it's not clear where you should start. At the end of the day, you have no clear idea of how you will spend the next day. This is a key strength found in high performers in information technology.

Skill 7: Organization

An easy clue to whether you are strong in Organization is how well you keep track of your belongings. If you're inclined to be neat and pay attention to detail, you most likely are strong in Organization, which is the ability to arrange according to a system. If your desk is generally tidy (and you naturally like it that way) and there are no piles of paper waiting to be filed, you're probably strong in Organization. If Organization is one of your strengths, everything has a place and you easily know where that place is.

If you're low in Organization, you're somewhat messy and routinely misplace or lose things. You don't maintain systems for organizing information, such as files, e-mail, or your in-box. You rely on others to find things you've misplaced. Everything does not have a normal place where it should be for you, and someone strong in Organization is likely to tell you where something goes.

Skill 8: Time Management

Time Management is the capacity to estimate how much time one has, to allocate it, and to stay within time limits and deadlines. It involves a sense that time is important. If you're strong in this skill, you tend to be efficient, able to meet deadlines, and methodical. When someone asks you how long it will take to complete a project, you can estimate the correct time within 90 percent accuracy. In the course of a day, you can juggle the tasks you need to accomplish so that most get completed and those that don't are the least important.

If you're weak in Time Management, you have difficulty meeting deadlines. The meetings you run don't start on time, run late, or often both. At the end of the day, you realize you didn't get done half of what you had planned because you consistently underestimated the amount of time it took to do something. You just *know* you can get somewhere at a certain time but never make it at that time. There's always a reason, be it traffic or weather, and frequently something took longer than expected.

Skill 9: Goal-Directed Persistence

If you succeed in most of the goals you set for yourself, you're probably strong in Goal-Directed Persistence, which is the capacity to have a goal and follow through with actions to achieve it. You can be expected to complete tasks you take on, and are able to define and achieve long-term goals. You don't let obstacles get in your way and always keep your eye on the ball, despite the efforts of those around you to draw you into activities unrelated to what you're trying to accomplish. You have the capacity to have a goal, follow through to the completion of the goal, and not be put off or distracted by competing interests.

If you tend to be controlled by the present, can't focus beyond the short term, and lose sight of objectives, you're probably weak in Goal-Directed Persistence. You typically can't turn down opportunities that pass your way, even when they prevent you from accomplishing important goals in a timely manner. You get excited by new ideas but can't seem to see them come to fruition.

Skill 10: Flexibility

Flexibility is the ability to revise plans, and it relates to the amount of adaptability one has to changing conditions. It involves the capacity to generate an alternative plan when confronted with obstacles or new information.

Being strong in Flexibility implies you're independent, able to integrate new information, adaptable and able to change course, and able to act autonomously. When your flight is canceled, you quickly work out alternative travel arrangements. When the overnight package needed for a meeting that day isn't delivered, you determine the best way to handle the situation without panicking. You can redo a presentation when an associate calls in sick at the last minute, and you can handle going back to school because your daughter left her homework assignment there. You have the ability to revise plans in the face of obstacles, setbacks, new information, or mistakes.

A low degree of Flexibility would make you less adaptable to change, with a lack of willingness to incorporate new information on the spot. Once you've decided on a plan, you're not comfortable changing it or seeing alternatives. You tend to panic when your car won't start, because you have an important meeting coming up, and you might get rattled when your boss asks you to make a change in your travel plans just after completing them with the travel agent. You are put out when someone calls while you're washing your car or the supermarket is out of a key ingredient you need for a planned dinner.

Skill 11: Metacognition

If you're self-reflective, think strategically, and are able to observe your own actions as well as group processes impartially, you're probably strong in Metacognition, which is the ability to stand back and take a bird's-eye view of yourself in a situation and be able to understand and make changes in how you solve problems. It's an ability to observe how you problem-solve and includes self-monitoring and self-evaluative skills, such as asking yourself, "How am I doing?" or "How did I do?" If Metacognition is one of your Executive Skills strengths, you can figure out multiple solutions to a problem, analyze the pros and cons of each, and select the one you think will work best. You can step back and figure out what went wrong in a failed presentation and can easily imagine the threats and opportunities of a new business venture.

A low skill of Metacognition means you don't think through the implications of decisions. You might be inclined to shoot from the hip, miss seeing the big picture, and tend to repeat the same mistakes. You make decisions based on what feels right and can make snap decisions about something that has long-term consequences you never thought of. You use the same approach to a problem even though that approach didn't work the last three times you used it. A clue that you are low in Metacognition is if people around you get annoyed with you for not being able to see what's important.

Skill 12: Stress Tolerance

This is the ability to thrive in stressful situations and to cope with uncertainty, change, and performance demands. If you're comfortable with the subjective feeling of stress and maintain control in pressure situations, you're probably strong in Stress Tolerance.

You'd have a high tolerance for ambiguity and be steady in a crisis. You can handle a deadline being moved up and even welcome the challenge of working through the night to finish it. Your children all have events the same evening, and you take it in stride that you have to get them to different locations on time.

Being low in Stress Tolerance would make you feel stressed in a crisis, and you only feel comfortable when you know your schedule for the next few weeks. If you make an error in a presentation, you're likely to obsess about it. You get angry when the boss asks you to divert from your current task in favor of another, or when your spouse asks you stop at a store on the way home just when you got on the highway.

Finding Your Own Strengths and Weaknesses

Of the 12 Executive Skills, each one is found in varying numbers of high performers. Where the particular Executive Skill is the high performer's strength, we expect it has been of value to his or her success because it likely is required for the job or functions that the person is performing. Where the skill is a weakness, it is not likely to be required because the person has been successful despite that weakness.

Executive Skills strengths and weaknesses are real and are imbedded in your brain. So saying you're strong in a particular Executive Skill does not make you strong in that skill (and you most likely will know it).

Additionally, there are people who delude themselves into thinking they're good at virtually everything, and they may tend to rate themselves as strong across the board. In clinical psychology, the term for intentionally viewing oneself in only positive terms in virtually every aspect across the board is called *faking good*. A person who is faking good will have difficulty admitting weaknesses.

Once you understand your own Executive Skills strengths and weaknesses, you likely will start to notice certain characteristics of those around you and how these skills come into play in day-to-day work situations. And even more significantly, once you identify the Executive Skills strengths found in high performers in particular positions or departments, you can potentially predict who might be more successful in that role in the future based on their own Executive Skills combinations. Of course, it's also important not to ignore the Executive Skills weaknesses because they can be a cause of potential problems.

Workload and Executive Skills

If there was never any pressure in day-to-day life, weak Executive Skills might not matter much. However, that's hardly ever the case at work. There are constant interactions, requirements to perform specific tasks and functions, and various pressures that come to bear on a regular basis. Many in business face daily pressures that make them live in highly stressful environments, which impact Executive Skills weaknesses.

Under pressure or stress, your weakest Executive Skills fail first. In essence, whatever your Executive Skills weaknesses, they become more pronounced. For example, if your weakest skill is, say, Task Initiation, when you are under a lot of pressure, you'll have difficulty starting anything. If your weakest skill is Sustained Attention, under a stressful condition it's likely you'll have even more difficulty staying focused on one topic or subject.

This is one of the reasons it's important to identify weaknesses as well as strengths. Because your weakest Executive Skills are always going to be your weakest, knowing them can help you watch for potential problems they may cause and avoid those situations.

And one of the causes of stress and pressure at work can be the sheer amount of work there is to do, so workload can play a significant role in how Executive Skills manifest themselves in the course of a day. Having too much to do puts pressure on your Executive Skills. The strengths are typically not an issue because they are just that, your strengths. It's the weaknesses that can be most impacted by workload.

And it turns out that the majority of senior executives and managers consider their personal workload and the workload of those around them to be too heavy (see Survey Results: Workload). When it comes to personal workload, most executives and managers say their workload is too heavy and the majority considers the sheer amount of work in their department to be too heavy. No one considers his personal workload to be significantly too light.

The larger the company, the more people say the workload in their department or organization is too heavy, with 92 percent of those at large organizations rating their personal workload as too heavy.

SURVEY RESULTS: WORKLOAD

In general, I consider the business workload (the sheer amount/volume of work) of people in my department and/or organization to be:

Significantly too heavy	17%
Somewhat too heavy	52%
About right	26%
Somewhat too light	4%
Significantly too light	1%

In general, I consider my personal workload today to be:

Significantly too heavy	26%
Somewhat too heavy	47%
About right	22%
Somewhat too light	4%
Significantly too light	0%

In general, I consider the business workload (the sheer amount/volume of work) of people in my department and/or organization to be:

	SMALL	MEDIUM	LARGE
Significantly too heavy	13%	19%	31%
Somewhat too heavy	50%	50%	62%
About right	31%	30%	5%
Somewhat too light	4%	2%	3%
Significantly too light	2%	0%	0%

Voices from the Front Lines: Workload

"The push for more revenue in a down-turning economy adds to the workload pressures."

"A key driver to effectively managing workload is the flexibility and ability to prioritize projects and communicating those priorities to the rest of the organization."

"Too many hats, not enough shoes."

"This is the most difficult time in 20 years regarding workload. Productivity is often being achieved by 'piling on' more work to the same amount of people. An insufficient amount of time is allowed for tasks."

"We are and have been in a position where we've had to do more with less. Therefore, one of our responsibilities as leaders is to surround ourselves with 'All Star' employees and not settle for mediocrity just to fill a chair."

"Workload is bordering on the absurd. Sixty- to seventy-hour weeks, travel on weekends, and giving back half of your vacation are commonplace."

"Expectations today are higher than they have ever been. Some days it's just too much."

"It's overwhelming and quite a challenge to manage others' expectations about what we are not willing to do."

"Do more with less still holds."

Fortunately for high performers, the volume of workload doesn't seem to be a significant issue because they're successful while still having certain Executive Skills weaknesses. There are several reasons for this, which we detail in a later chapter. In some cases, their strengths could compensate for their weaknesses, or their specific Executive Skills weaknesses are skills not really necessary for success in their particular role. We highlight these specific strengths and weaknesses by multiple categories throughout the book.

Exceeding Your Cognitive Bandwidth

Beyond the volume of workload, there's another aspect of Executive Skills involving what we call your cognitive bandwidth. If someone you know (or you) is struggling with overload and feels like she's losing it, on the edge, not able to remember things, and totally stressed out, she may have reached the end of her cognitive bandwidth. While the person has a built-in capacity to meet complex challenges and opportunities through the use of the functions of the prefrontal cortex of the brain, there can be times when too much information overloads the system. There's nothing necessarily wrong with the person; it's just that the actual amount of information she's attempting to handle or process through the 12 brain functions has exceeded the capacity of those functions. This causes the person's frontal lobes to effectively break down.

Symptoms of such a breakdown could be feeling overwhelmed, having trouble planning the day, or having a feeling that there's so much to do you don't even know where to begin. You also might see it at home, in instances such as finding yourself screaming at your children or spouse for something that at other times would be considered trivial. Exceeding cognitive bandwidth occurs when information load exceeds information capacity. Your Executive Skills, which are required to manage the information in the brain, just can't handle the volume, speed, or complexity, or a combination of all three. The information to which you have access can exceed your hardwired or cognitive ability to manage it.

We know from psychological and neuropsychological research that information overload degrades Executive Skills. And when Executive Skills fail under pressure, the weakest skills fail first. When the amount of information coming in exceeds cognitive bandwidth, the result is that decision-making speed and accuracy can suffer and mistakes increase.

Fatigue also lowers the threshold as your weakest Executive Skills begin to fail, in which case you can also exceed your cognitive bandwidth. You can simply become too tired or exhausted from working too many long hours over a period of time or working long hours under nonstop pressure. You can probably remember a time when you simply felt too tired to make a logical or complex decision, so you put it off for another time. You might have had a breakdown in your Executive Skills due to fatigue.

Exceeding your cognitive bandwidth can grow out of information overload, which happens because information is so freely flowing. Not all information has to be dealt with, and much of it can passively be ignored. However, information overload can evolve into exceeding cognitive bandwidth when much of the information is relevant or you attempt to deal with most or all of it. Information is flowing at you nonstop, from your laptop, phone, cell phone, and PDA. You can easily exceed cognitive bandwidth by treating all information you receive as of equal importance.

In a similar fashion, stress also has a detrimental effect on Executive Skills. Stress creates unnecessary "noise" or clutter in the brain's information-processing systems and decreases the capacity to manage information. While Executive Skills such as Sustained Attention and Working Memory are highly vulnerable to stress, we've noticed another significant effect: Stress is most likely to have a negative impact on your weakest skills. This means that the Executive Skills that already are a struggle for you will decline further when you're subjected to too much information or increased stress.

This decline in a skill can actually serve as a barometer, indicating that you're overloaded or experiencing excessive stress. For example, if you're already weak in Organization and start to feel even more disorganized, or look that way to others, this is often a sign that you're trying to handle too many demands or are overly stressed. Or if you're low in Flexibility and Emotion Control and begin to feel or show increased frustration, irritability, or even anger, this can be a signal that you're overloaded.

When you exceed your cognitive bandwidth, logical decisions can't be made because Executive Skills are needed to execute. Without them, you won't be able to prioritize, manage emotions, deal with the bigger picture, and function effectively.

When your Executive Skills aren't working well due to exceeding your cognitive bandwidth, you're experiencing what is called Executive Skills dysfunction. The good news is that your cognitive bandwidth can be increased by increasing efficiency. Interestingly, young adults who have grown up processing multiple streams of information simultaneously in many ways already may be more adept at handling more simultaneous information because they've developed those skills naturally throughout their youth. However, even they have limitations in their cognitive bandwidth. How much information you can process before reaching the end of your cognitive bandwidth will be obvious to you, as well as to those around you when it happens.

The key step to avoid reaching maximum cognitive bandwidth is to select and prioritize information. Critical to this selection process is establishing priorities for types of information, so that not all information is viewed as being equal. You have to essentially turn off some sources of information, or at least ignore some.

Exceeding cognitive bandwidth is a very real thing in business today, and there's no shortage of stress as a result. Four out of five managers and executives say they're stressed at work, with a third being highly stressed.[1] Ironically, Executive Skills are needed for decision making, and the more stressed you are, the less you can make strong decisions.

Knowing in Advance

So once you've identified your Executive Skills strengths and weaknesses, it's much easier to predict where issues may arise, both positively and negatively. By knowing your strengths, for example, it's easier to know which positions would likely be more natural for you based on the strengths most needed for that function. The strengths of high performers in our study can also help you better match yourself with specific industries, departments, and titles based on your own Executive Skills strengths.

Knowing weaknesses also can help identify which positions or functions are likely to be unnatural or difficult for you, based on your weaknesses being the strengths required for a particular job or function. The results of our study should help you there as well, as you'll see in later chapters. And by being able to identify the strengths and weaknesses of others, you can see how to better position them for success as well.

Executive Skills are not something you or others can learn or develop as an adult because they're essentially built-in since birth, and we will discuss the science behind them in the next chapter.

2

Finding Success and Avoiding Failure

Why Your Strengths and Weaknesses Are the Way They Are: The Science Behind Executive Skills

ONCE YOU understand Executive Skills, it becomes quite obvious how they play out in business and work environments. If you're consistently late, you can pretty accurately surmise you're weak in Time Management. If you seem to daydream after a few minutes of a colleague or your boss speaking to you, you're likely weak in Sustained Attention. And if you always seem to get the long-term project done on time no matter what, you're likely strong in Goal-Directed Persistence.

Over the past few years, in our presentations at large events as well as smaller seminars, we've described each of these skills to thousands of businesspeople. The reaction from businesspeople is typically very positive. Once they understand Executive Skills strengths and weaknesses, savvy businesspeople better grasp what it is that they've been facing, in some cases, for years. They just never had a template to use, that template being the 12 Executive Skills.

So how do high-performing individuals end up in the right jobs? It could be that for various reasons they ended up in work situations that play to their Executive Skills strengths. It could be that they instinctively know what they're good at and seek out such situations. It could be that someone above them has identified certain traits in these individuals and purposefully moved them into positions that play to those strengths. It also could just be plain luck of people landing in positions that are so suited to their strengths that they become high performers.

Whatever the reason people end up in the right situation, Executive Skills strengths can be matched to high-performing people in business, with certain skills found in some situations more than in others.

Another reaction we occasionally receive from people is that these skills can be changed. A typical exchange might go something like this:

"I don't believe that these skills are not changeable in people."

"Okay. Tell me of a case where you 'fixed' someone."

"I do it all the time, and have throughout my career."

"Okay, give me the details of just one case."

"I had someone who worked for me who just couldn't finish projects on time and I fixed that."

"That's great. How did you fix it?"

"Easy. I had that person partner with another employee who always finishes on time, and now they do the projects together and are always on time."

The manager may perceive that he "fixed" or changed a person's Executive Skill (in this case, likely low Goal-Directed Persistence), but he actually changed the situation so that the low Executive Skill no longer caused a problem. Many successful business leaders have devised various "fixes" for situations but not really for changing Executive Skills strengths or weaknesses.

For example, in a two-day seminar I conducted with attendees from a wide range of companies, one of the individuals on the first day said he did not believe that Executive Skills were not changeable. From experience over a period of years, we've come to realize that different people come to accept this in different time frames, and some might never. We can't make people believe it (even though it is true); we can only describe it to them, give examples, and show the benefits of improving interactions. So at the beginning of this seminar, we described how each person typically has that "aha" moment in his or her own time frame—sometimes immediately, sometimes after a few hours, or days, or even weeks or months. Early in the program on the second day, this person abruptly interrupted the class to say he had just had his "aha" moment. Like the other attendees, he was completing a profile of a subordinate and it just struck this person that he had given this subordinate essentially the same performance review over a period of seven years. He had been trying to correct the same Executive Skills weakness for seven straight years. "I just realized I'm never going to change this person," he said.

While these exchanges are from the business marketplace, knowledge of Executive Skills in that area is relatively new, having been introduced primarily through our previous book, *SMARTS: Are We Hardwired for Success?* However, knowledge of the origins of these skills dates back decades in psychology, and they have been studied extensively and are well documented, from their development at birth through to behaviors associated with them.

Executive Skills in Psychology

Humans have a built-in capacity to meet challenges and accomplish goals through the use of these high-level cognitive functions known as Executive Skills. These skills help you decide what activities or tasks to pay attention to and which ones you will choose to do.[1]

They allow you to organize your behavior over time and override immediate demands in favor of longer-term goals. Through the use of these skills you can plan and organize activities, sustain attention, and persist to complete a task. Executive Skills enable you to manage emotions and monitor thoughts in order to work more efficiently and effectively. They essentially help you regulate your behavior.

Executive Skills and the Brain

Executive Skills are built-in, existing in the brain as potential from birth but not developing for some time after that. Much like language, Executive Skills lie dormant in the brain as future skills.

Assuming that there's no insult to the brain and that experience is reasonably normal, these skills unfold over time. As they unfold, they are influenced by the genes you inherit from your parents as well as by the biological and social environment in which you live. If the parents did not have good organization or attention skills, chances are increased that the son or daughter will have Executive Skills problems.

If someone is raised in a biologically or socially toxic environment, such as one with lead exposure or psychological trauma, there's an increased likelihood that Executive Skills will suffer. Otherwise, Executive Skills begin to develop and show themselves soon after birth in a slow progression to full adult development.

The beginnings of Executive Skills can be seen in infants and toddlers and even more in five-year-olds. But even in a 15-year-old, there still can be the lack of planning, time management, or especially inhibition. So these skills, which are at the heart of self-regulation or self-control, begin to develop in early infancy and continue to develop well into adolescence and early adulthood.

Executive Skills reach a reasonable level of development only by mid- to-late adolescence or later. This is when relevant adults (parents, teachers, employers) begin to feel more confidence in the self-regulatory ability of the teenager. This increased confidence is reflected in the choices and opportunities that are made available, such as driver's licenses, less restricted work hours, course selection, and credit cards. Prior to this development, adults help compensate for incomplete development by essentially lending their frontal lobes or Executive Skills to the child.

This happens in one of two ways. The first is direct, coming in the form of directives, limits, and rules. For example, in the toddler who has little impulse control, moving toward potential danger typically leads to a sharp "No!" Or for the young child who is unable to make and follow a plan, the adults construct the plan and then prompt or cue each step, not completing the task for the child but assuring that with help the child will be successful. In effect, they are a surrogate frontal lobe that operates for the child as a set of supplementary Executive Skills. But even adults sometimes rely on the Executive Skills of others to help compensate for their own weaknesses. We suspect that in the case of some high-performing individuals in business, this is the case—and perhaps some of the reason behind their success.

The second method involves structuring the environment in a way that compensates for underdeveloped skills. For adolescents, parents gate off as best they can access to alcohol, drugs, and weapons, and the adolescents are held in a controlled environment (school) where their options only gradually expand. This model is not universal, but it certainly prevails in Western cultures (and gradually emerges in developing countries). Some of these environmental modifications continue into adulthood, with businesses establishing deadlines, job descriptions, and work rules to ensure that people are not relying solely on their own Executive Skills to manage performance expectations.

Executive Skills and Brain Development

The development of Executive Skills over the first 20 or so years of life parallels the development of the brain and specific brain systems over that time. At birth, a child's brain weighs about 400 grams. By late adolescence, it has increased to about 1,400 grams,[2] or from 10 to 12 ounces to a little over three pounds. A number of changes in the brain account for this significant growth. Broadly speaking, growth of the brain over the course of development occurs through the generation of nerve cells (neurons) and their supporting cells (neuroglia). These cells are the building blocks of the nervous system. In order for nerve cells to talk with each other, they develop branches called axons and dendrites, which allow them to send and receive information from other cells.

When psychologists talk about the material that makes up the brain—neurons, dendrites, axons, and the like—they think about this in terms of shadings of the brain: gray and white matter. The white matter acquires its shading through a process called myelination and represents bundles of axons that connect different regions of the brain and allow them to communicate. (Not to get too technical, but myelin is a fatty sheath that forms around the axon and provides insulation that helps increase the speed of transmission of nerve signals. So the conversations—as nerve signals—carried on by axons between neurons are made more efficient by this process of insulation.)

Myelination begins in the earliest stages of development and in the frontal lobes continues well into late adolescence or young adulthood. This process is one of the key features of frontal lobe development, and the time course of this process parallels the time course and development of Executive Skills.

Gray matter comprises nerve cells or neurons and the connections between them, which are called synapses. The development of gray matter is a bit more complex than that of myelin, as it involves a series of increases followed by reductions. For example, it is estimated that the fetal brain, at five months, has about 100 billion neurons. This is comparable to the number of neurons in the average adult brain. And in early childhood, the number of synapses (about a quadrillion) greatly exceeds the number in the adult brain. If the development of gray matter continued at this pace, the adult brain would be enormous.

Instead, a different phenomenon occurs. There's an initial increase in gray matter (neurons and particularly synapses) in early childhood. This increase peaks before age five and then there's a gradual reduction or pruning of these connections. The initial increase occurs during a period of rapid learning and experience in early childhood. Recent brain research suggests that as this learning and skill development becomes more efficient, additional increases in gray matter could actually undermine new learning. The pruning process allows the child to consolidate skills, and the gray matter connections that are not needed or used drop away. This period of consolidation continues until a second period of significant growth in gray matter that begins around age 11 or 12, the beginning of another period recognized for rapid learning and development. This increase is again followed by a period of reduction through pruning over the course of adolescence.

Research indicates that this growth spurt in the brain prior to adolescence occurs primarily in the frontal lobes. It's as if the brain is preparing itself both for the development of Executive Skills and for the significant demands that will be made on Executive Skills during adolescence and adulthood. Researchers at the National Institute of Mental Health also suggest that a "use-it-or-lose-it" process may be occurring in the frontal lobes during this time. Neural connections that are used are retained, while those not exercised are lost. If this is the case, then the practice of these skills is important not only for learning self-management, but also for the development of brain structures that will support these skills into later adolescence and adulthood.

Researchers now generally agree that frontal brain systems (the frontal/prefrontal cortex along with connections to adjacent areas) make up the neurological base for Executive Skills. Figure 2–1 depicts the human brain with the approximate location of major functions, including Executive Skills in the prefrontal cortex.

We do not mean to oversimplify or suggest that the prefrontal cortex is the only area of the brain related to Executive Skills. Recent neuroimaging evidence suggests that other areas of the brain also are involved.[3] Nonetheless, the prefrontal cortex and nearby associated systems play a preeminent role in the relationship between brain structure and executive function.

Prefrontal brain systems are among the last to fully develop, in late adolescence and early adulthood, and they are the final, common pathway for

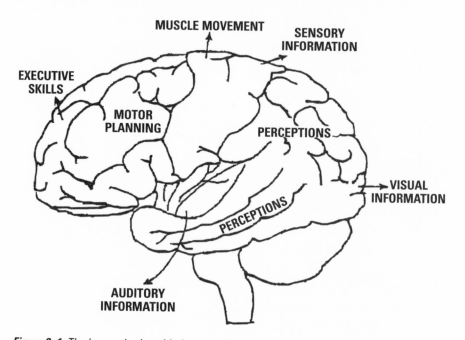

Figure 2–1. The human brain, with the approximate location of major functions. Photo and some material in this chapter have been adapted with permission from Chapter 1 of *Exectuive Skills in Children and Adolescents*, 2/e, by Peg Dawson and Richard Guare, The Guilford Press, New York, 2010.

managing information and behavior from other brain regions. Hart and Jacobs[4] have summarized the critical functions of the frontal lobes in the management of information and behavior:

- The frontal lobes decide what is worth attending to and what is worth doing.

- The frontal lobes provide continuity and coherence to behavior across time.

- The frontal lobes modulate affective and interpersonal behaviors so that drives are satisfied within the constraints of the internal and external environments.

- The frontal lobes monitor, evaluate, and adjust.

Executive Skills are intimately tied to the frontal lobes and more broadly to frontal brain systems. This relationship can help explain how Executive Skills develop over the course of childhood and adolescence and move into adulthood. Goldberg has compared the frontal lobes and particularly the prefrontal cortex to the roles that the CEO plays in a corporation, the general takes in an army, and the conductor performs in an orchestra.[5]

For most people, Executive Skills and the underlying brain structures that support them are developed by young adulthood. By the time you reach your mid-20s, your patterns of Executive Skills, both strengths and weaknesses, are established. These patterns persist throughout most of adult life. By identifying the Executive Skills of high performers based on what they do and where they work, our intent is to help you determine perfect-fit situations in advance, whether for you or for those you manage.

Barring injuries or illnesses that impact the brain or processes later in life, such as dementia, your Executive Skills will remain relatively unchanged from young adulthood through retirement years. This fact has significant implications for all aspects of business life.

Although people may be able to make minor modifications in their skills through training and experience, significant changes will not happen. For example, strengths in Time Management will remain strengths, and weaknesses in Flexibility will remain weaknesses. Because the skills will not change, if people are to succeed at work and life, they need to find a fit between their patterns of strengths and weaknesses and their work and living situations.

If you take on jobs that demand skill patterns that are significantly different from your own, frustration and failure are likely. On the other hand, if you can identify your Executive Skills patterns and understand what skills are demanded by certain jobs or careers, you can maximize the likelihood of success in a job and, at the same time, be aware of where you'll need to compensate for weaknesses. The same is true in matching the skills patterns of people you manage and matching those patterns to jobs and functions that best suit those strengths. Identifying the Executive Skills of high-performing individuals should facilitate that process, for both yourself and those you deal with.

The first step to do that, which many businesses, executives, and managers have already taken, is to determine the criteria for how you and your organization determine who is a high-performing individual. The executives and managers in our study had little difficulty in determining their high performers in all cases, as you'll see in the next chapter. By seeing how others identify who is a high-performing individual, you can use some of the same criteria to determine how your organization defines high performers and establish if you fit their criteria.

You also can compare what criteria are used at other organizations to the criteria used by yours. This may give you a clearer path for you to become a high performer within your company, if you aren't already. It also can show you how other people have become successful, based on how their Executive Skills match the criteria used to determine who's a high performer in their organizations. The insight of how others determine the criteria for high performance also may provide you with new or additional measures to use within your own organization if you're in a position to determine who's a high performer there.

Additionally, the criteria may give you a better understanding of the detailed results of the study when we compare those criteria to the Executive Skills strengths of the high performers in certain jobs.

3

What Is a High Performer and How Do You Become One?

Selecting the Right Path to Increase the Chance of Success

IF YOU ASK typical managers to identify their high-performing individuals, they know right away who they are. They name them based on a range of criteria including performance, experience, attitude, corporate metrics, and subjectivity. Many large organizations have relatively sophisticated and quantitative metrics, as you might expect, while medium and smaller businesses use a slightly smaller number of formulas or metrics, though they all can easily determine their high performers.

If you stop and think for a moment, you probably can identify who you think are the high-performing people in your department or organization. You may consider yourself to be one, in which case your Executive Skills may be a match for your current job. Or if you don't consider yourself to be a high performer, perhaps your Executive Skills don't match your current position. However, you may have the Executive Skills strengths that could propel you to be a high performer in a different role, organization, or even industry.

In any case, it's typically not a large percentage of people in any given area who are high performers, no matter which criteria are used, and business leaders in our study provided a wide variety of methods they use to determine high performers.

Once you see how a wide range of businesses determine what factors make a high performer, you may see a potential path for you to follow, especially once you see how specific Executive Skills match the specific high-performance criteria. And if you manage others, this information can help you determine the best paths for those people to get them in situations that give them a better chance of being a high performer.

Performance-Based: Consistency Is Key

Many managers select high performers based on actual performance. For example, one credit union selected 19 high performers based on "overall job performance, dedication to the credit union, and focus on strengthening the credit union to include team building." The CEO of a creative advertising agency selects his high performers as those who "consistently contribute an extremely high-quality product/output and do so in a timely and efficient manner. In addition, these individuals possess a high degree of capacity and competency in their jobs." Another CEO defines his high performer as "someone who consistently exceeds expectations in their work."

In some cases, the selection is based on traditional performance reviews over a period of time. Geri Rhoades, vice president of organizational development at Cafco, a construction management company in Boston, says she looks for "the individuals with an exceptional performance review history, reputation in the organization as high performers, and agreements from their managers as being high performers."[1]

Lori McLeese, chief people officer of Room to Read in San Francisco, selects high performers based on those who received the top two scores on performance reviews last year, which she equates to delivering results and "working in a way that exemplifies our core values, and takes a leadership role in the organization."[2]

Executives and managers at several participating organizations easily recall recent performance reviews of their high performers. "The criteria I used included those with exceptional performance reviews this past year, those that are exceedingly competent with their job, those that demonstrate strong initiative and follow through, and those that I count on to get every job done," says Tom Ortner, executive director of Willow Glen Care Center.[3]

The human resources director of a California organization determines high performers based on the results they repeatedly achieve for the organization. They are primarily the employees who consistently received above-average ratings on performance reviews.

In other cases, the selection is more subjective, based on personal knowledge and experience over a period of time. "Having worked in communications at ICMA for more than 22 years, I feel safe saying that I am in tune with which of my colleagues would be generally considered high performers versus which ones would not," says Michele Frisby, director of public information at the International City/County Management Association (ICMA), a Washington, D.C.–based professional and educational organization for chief appointed managers, administrators, and assistants in cities, towns, and counties, as well as regional entities around the world.[4] "For the record, however, I tapped those individuals who I felt were super productive and performed consistently at a high level."

This consistency over time as well as track record played some role in a large number of those identifying high performers. One selected those "able to excel where others have failed and who continuously complete tasks, plan successfully, and are on time, meeting budgetary requirements."

Close knowledge of subordinates also plays a role in high-performer identification, with some executives selecting their direct reports, since they know only high performers could succeed in those particular positions.

It is obvious that management overall has specific expectations of high performers and clear benchmarks in advance to determine if certain targets have been met. The concept of being a high performer in an organization was hardly nebulous, as managers quickly identify those who stand above the rest. And they always know why.

For example, Nancy Benullo, the footwear product director in the Ryka division of American Sporting Goods, has specific criteria to determine her high performers, who all work in various functional areas of the athletic footwear industry.[5] Her criteria include an overall focus on consistency:

- Consistently meets or exceeds sales goals

- Consistently meets or exceeds profitability goals

- Consistently contributes to bottom-line profitability by design-ing/developing marketable performance athletic footwear

- Consistently contributes to bottom-line profitability by directing the design, development, and marketing process of an exclusive product line for national retail accounts

It also does not seem to matter where high performers physically work day in and day out; they are always easy to identify. At Tri-Global Solutions, a management consulting company in Alberta, Canada, many of the top performers work outside the office at client sites (at management levels) rather than hold executive positions within the company.[6] Sandra Lambert of Tri-Global identifies high performers as those who:

- Consistently exceed customer expectations or other performance measures

- Have demonstrated the ability to deliver products or services that are above average in quality and value

- Exemplify corporate values including professionalism, integrity, and customer-focused service

"Essentially, our top-performers are those individuals who provide highest value both by enhancing corporate reputation and generating rev-enue in return for the organization's investment in them," Lambert says.

Quantitative: Expectations and Results

Your organization may be like many others that look at high performers as those who deliver precise results, by a range of methods, many with detailed measurement metrics.

"I identify high performers from the home plant and from corporate as those who are positive, forward thinking, and seem to always get results," says Howard Elton, technical manager at Rhodia, an international chemicals company headquartered in Vernon, Texas.[7] "Typically, I notice that these people exhibit more intelligence in their specific area, but also the ability to apply an equal level of intelligence across a broader range of subjects. They seem to be able to connect the dots better than most."

In one sales organization whose primary mission is sales lead generation and appointment setting for companies in the technology area, the top performers were determined simply by monthly lead point average (LPA). The high performers who participated had the highest LPA for the previous month.

Higher-I.T., a California-based company that specializes in matching healthcare IT talent with healthcare organizations, like many other organizations, uses specific metrics to determine high performers. "I use very simple criteria to determine our high performers: target vs. actual, measured results in three areas: net profits, business volume/expansion, and customer satisfaction," says company president Don Boatright.[8] There is no doubt as to results, since all areas can be quantitatively measured.

The head of an organization that services nonprofit insurance businesses also uses straightforward measures to determine who the high performers are. "The high performers we select are my senior managers, who, individually and as a team, consistently meet and frequently exceed my expectations," says Pamela Davis, president and CEO of Alliance Member Services.[9] "The senior managers identify individuals within their departments that meet those definitions."

The assistant vice president of business affairs at one state university identifies high performers by financial management, people management, the ability to change to conditions in the work environment, the ability to think strategically, and the ability to see the big picture.

Qualitative: Some Subjectivity

Some organizations have somewhat more subjective or relaxed methods of identifying their high performers, though managers there also are quick to say who they are.

"The criteria used to determine the high performers were people that I work with closely every day who are continuously seen as the best managers in our division," says Nancy Reinhardt of the New Jersey Civil Rights

Department.[10] "They are confident and creative in dealing with issues that come up within the units they manage and they are quick to recognize when their staff needs direct guidance to complete tasks on time. It also helps that they enjoy their work, and I believe it contributes to their success."

James Bartlett, executive director of the North Dakota Home School Association, identifies his high performers as those who "push the envelope toward progress," while Brooke Frost, the executive director of Big Brothers Big Sisters of Central California, sees them as "those with initiative and a strong work ethic, [who] present well in public (both written and in person) and meet goals, while maintaining or exceeding standards of performance."[11]

Several executives mentioned that high performers frequently exceed what is expected of them, that they tend to do more than is required of them. For example, at the Bridges Resort and Tennis Club in Warren, Vermont, high performers are considered "employees who go above and beyond their jobs," says Laina Aylward, administrative assistant and director of homeowner services at the resort.[12] "They take on extra work if needed, they help in other departments, [and] they care about the people they work with and our clients and are always looking for ways to improve our services."

At Trinity Counseling Center, a division of Trinity College of Graduate Studies, high performers are identified as those who are "self-directed, collaborative, creative and successful in meeting and adapting goals," says Florence Bishop, executive director of the program.[13] "They convey personal satisfaction and enjoyment in the process of their work."

As you'll see later in the book, many of these characteristics of high performers match certain Executive Skills strengths, especially when comparing the strengths of the high performers to the actual titles they hold.

Position in the Organization

Some organizations determine their high performers based on positions held in the organization. For example, one national retailer selected all high-level managers while another selected the CEO, CFO, chief of staff, and several vice presidents. Yet another company chose the five heads of the company—the president, treasurer, director of engineering, department head, and partner—then included the director of marketing and focused on the project managers who lead teams of engineers.

The thinking there goes that if a person holds a certain position or has a particularly significant role to play in the business, that person has to be a high-performing individual just to hold that position. One hospital, for example, identified its executive team since each of those members was chosen by the CEO. One region of a well-known nationwide bank selected high performers based on titles of business development and sales managers, since each is responsible for overall accountability of a certain bank branch. If those managers are not high-performing, they are not likely to retain that position over time.

At the United Kingdom operation of Esselte, the world's leading global office supplies manufacturer, Mark Katz, chief information officer (CIO), considers his direct reports and key managers to be the high performers.[14] "I do consider all of them reasonably high-performing staff," says Katz. "I must admit, this is a bit selfish since I wanted to really use the survey as a benchmark of my own team against others."

George Brennan, executive vice president of sales and marketing at Interstate Hotels and Resorts, selected whom he considered to be "two of the highest achieving executives in the company. Both have reported to me and have been promoted to senior vice president positions of important responsibility in our company."[15]

One federal governmental agency selected a team leader and the division and branch chiefs as well as the budget acquisition office and data management office leaders, while a maintenance team leader selected the director of engineering, director of quality, maintenance manager, purchasing manager, and productions manager.

Greg D. Johnson, president of Euro RSCG Edge, identified high performers as the ten presidents, CFOs, and leaders within the Euro family of agencies. "The criteria I used was that they must all be in leadership roles and got there before the age of 40," says Johnson.[16]

At SUN Home Health Services in Northumberland, Pennsylvania, Finance Vice President David A. Miller selects high performers based on them being "anyone who is in a manager, director, or vice president position,"[17] while Procedyne in New Brunswick, New Jersey, identifies its high performers as those who are recognized managers, vice presidents, the CEO, and the COO.

The selection of high performers also goes beyond holding a certain title, as many look at their stars as those who are shown to cause specific impact to their organizations. For example, the vice president of finance at one company identifies high performers as those in a position to alter the direction of the company by their decisions and actions.

One organization determined its high performers based on those who manage a program or supervise staff, since they recently went through an intense strategic planning process to determine that these are the emerging leaders, and one bank simply selected as high performers the three highest-ranking officers at the bank.

The director of curriculum, instruction, and assessment at one education institution determined his high performers to be the superintendent, business administrator, student services director, principals, and assistants at each of the schools, while the director of academic technology at a university identified high performers as those who have risen to senior positions in their careers.

Company First

While many organizations use rather concrete terms to select their high performers, others focus on a sense of contribution to the overall good of the organization. The vice president of sales of a transportation company identifies his high performers based on those who are "intensely dedicated to their work and always looking out for the interests of the company and its personnel, long and short term. They are highly energetic and open-minded toward new ideas and toward future operations. They are well regarded and respected by others in their industry, both personally and professionally."

During the course of the study, many pointed to intangibles beyond quantitative results. For example, the manager at one of the largest banks in the United States selects her high performers based on "quarterly performance reviews and amount of annual bonus, as it is performance based; the highest dollars going to the best performers." Meanwhile, the executive vice president of a national association defined his high performers as "self-starters needing little or no supervision; restless, creative managers always looking for new projects to take on and master; and determined leaders who get jobs done on time and within budget."

Doing more than asked was a recurring theme heard throughout the study. One business leader identified his high performers as "simply folks who I can rely on to get things done with minimal fuss and who are always willing to go the extra mile."

Sue Miller, vice president of knowledge development at the Wisconsin Automobile and Truck Dealers Association, defines her high performers as those who "are self-motivated, strive to be ethical and courteous with everyone, highly productive (high speed and accuracy), whose behavior does not change substantially under stress, is highly respected by subordinates as well as peers, and is likeable."[18]

At one division of Cardinal Health, the $87 billion global manufacturer and distributor of medical supplies and technologies, making a particular area better is what counts. The company defines high performers as key people within a department with the know-how and abilities required to not only perform current operations, but also to improve upon them and implement changes for their department "to achieve and exceed their goals and discover and implement new opportunities."

At Verso Paper, a Memphis, Tennessee–based supplier of coated papers to the catalog, magazine, and commercial print markets, high performers are those who are "engaged" in the business. "They are interested and involved in making our company a better, more viable company," says Darlene Marstaller in the company's human resources department.[19] She says that the high performers there look for ways to be involved in the day-to-day business. "They are committed employees who volunteer for additional tasks and responsibility within their departments and within the mill," she says. "They look for ways to make our process more efficient and they readily share ideas. If our supervisors were asked to rank order their employees from their best to their worst, the high performers would rank one of the best, if not *the* best, employees in the department."

Indeed, several executives and managers pointedly looked to the overall benefit that high performers provide to the organization rather than to themselves as key to a longer-term future for that high performer.

For example, Dawn Harris, executive vice president and chief operating officer of Campus Federal Credit Union in Baton Rouge, Louisiana, whose Executive Skills strengths include Metacognition and Flexibility,

says there is a distinction between high performers. She sees high performers as being in two categories: those who may perform for their own
personal gain and those who perform for the greater good of the organization.[20] Says Harris:

> In thinking about those in our organization who would be consid-
> ered high-performing individuals, the thing that struck me was that
> there are individuals who could seem like the perfect executive.
> However, the question that remains is the reason why they do the
> things they do.
>
> Some high-performing individuals may do it from the standpoint
> of their own individual goals rather than goals that are in the best
> interest of the organization. If the high performers cannot reconcile
> their own personal interests with those of the organization, then they
> may have a short, very successful career economically and move on.
> This hinders the organization's ability to perform succession plan-
> ning and can be damaging to the corporate culture. The high per-
> former must be replaced, and the time, effort, and assimilation of
> that replacement may not successfully integrate the new individual
> into a current or future executive role. Additionally, if the individual
> wreaks havoc on a department, causing dissension and interpersonal
> conflict, then the good economic work they have done may be over-
> shadowed by the decline in morale they caused.
>
> Small companies in a co-operative world, such as ours, have two
> distinct groups of stakeholders: our member-owners and our staff.
> The new buzz phrase in human resource circles seems to be
> employee engagement. Yet the role that coinciding organizational
> and individual values/goals play in this engagement seems to be
> glossed over. This could be a part of the emotional engagement that
> plays a part, but still, it seems that the truly high-performing indi-
> vidual in any position can only be successful from the organization's
> standpoint if they stay to help develop the organization's corporate
> culture and conquer task/project activities that provide economic
> success. It is interesting to note that there are individuals who believe
> they are tactful, diplomatic, keep their cool, etc. in the workplace.

However, their departments receive poor scores for internal service surveys, and they themselves also score poorly. The department is a reflection of them, so do you want them—high performers that they are—to be an executive in the company? Probably not.

It seems that the highest performers (the most successful executives) have been able to reconcile their company's mission with their own mission in life. Whether the executive's success is defined by industry recognition, expanded economic success, societal position, or simply their own feeling of self-worth and value, those who truly believe in their company build a corporate culture that includes a staff of like believers. They are the ones that a company truly wants as their leader because it will lead to sustainability—not so much unbridled profitability, but company longevity, which is the key to success.

Multidimensional

Many organizations identify their high performers with multidimensions, those possessing some of one trait and some of another. No matter the organization type or size, the characteristics to select high performers had similarities. In discussing their high performers, many point to their abilities to lead or influence others.

Patrick F. Murphy, senior vice president of implementation service at ING, a global financial services company, looks for "excellent communication skills, the ability to objectively communicate information, people who think on their feet and give their teams clear direction. These are all characteristics we use to identify high performers. I also look for creative problem solvers—people who can see the bigger, strategic picture without losing sight of the tactical issue at hand."[21]

Chris Harper, dean of academic affairs at Pinkerton Academy, the largest independent academy in the United States, identifies his high performers as creative risk takers who, while being good managers, are able to be leaders and move the institution forward.[22]

Jim Doyle, partner and electronics industry solutions leader for the Americas at IBM Global Business Services, identifies high performers as top members of his sales team. "In terms of criteria used to determine top performers, it is fairly straightforward," says Doyle.[23] "It is actual sales versus plan (quantitative), sales of associated IBM products and services (not directly measured on, but good for IBM overall) and peer feedback (qualitative). Roughly the top five to ten percent receive top ratings, and on my team you are not eligible for top rating unless you exceed plan."

At the O'Hanlon Center for the Arts in Mill Valley, California, high performers are considered to be those who routinely set and meet short- and long-term goals, those who create change toward organizational evolution, and those who are able to detach personal ego when necessary but also know when to employ their personal skills, says Executive Director Megan Wilkinson.[24]

Jeri Shumate, executive director of 211info in Portland, Oregon, also uses a multidimensional approach, and defines high performers as those who:

- Are willing to own the responsibilities inherent in their job description

- Are able to think independently and make decisions confidently, without needing approval, unless appropriate

- Are able to see the long-term (and even short-term) implications of making a decision one way or another

- Are willing to put in a moderate amount of extra time if needed in order to accomplish a goal

- Accomplish noticeably more in a regular workday than others in the same position

"It's interesting that we have a really powerful team of workers here, yet that I would still consider most of them good performers rather than high performers," says Shumate.[25] "They give of their hearts and souls but don't necessarily accomplish above and beyond the average level of performance."

The head of one educational institution identifies high performers as high achievers who have the willingness to expand their sphere of influence and reflect on their professional practice as markers for high achievement.

How Many Are High Performers?

Another challenge was to determine how many people in business are true high-performing individuals, or at least perceived to be, by either themselves or those for whom they work. It turns out that the overwhelming majority of senior executives and managers consider themselves to be high performers (see Survey: Number of High Performers). That did not surprise us, since in today's business climate, in many cases holding significant management positions is possible only by performing at high levels.

But managers' views of themselves are quite different from their views of others in their department or organization. The majority of executives and managers consider fewer than half of those around them to be high-performing individuals, with almost 60 percent saying that fewer than a quarter are high-performing. Only one in five business leaders considers more than half of the people in his or her department or organization to be high performers. These estimates were born out during the study, as executives and managers with a wide range of titles identified relatively small percentages of their colleagues and subordinates as high-performing individuals. But the managers also frequently identify their high performers as the go-to people to get things done. They know who is a high performer and who is not, and it appears most are not, at least in their eyes.

SURVEY: NUMBER OF HIGH PERFORMERS

"In general, how many of the people in your department and/or organization would you consider to be high-performing individuals?"

1–5%	11%
6–10%	17%
11–15%	11%
16–20%	8%
21–25%	12%
26–30%	5%
31–35%	4%
36–40%	3%

41–45%	1%
46–50%	8%
51% or more	21%

"I consider myself to be a high-performing individual"

Strongly agree	63%
Somewhat agree	33%
Neither agree nor disagree	3%
Somewhat disagree	1%
Strongly disagree	0%

Voices from the Front Lines: Number of High Performers

"I know a lot of people consider themselves as High Performers. However, I think everyone has room for improvement. Our corporation has started to limit the number of those folks rated as high performer or leading. The problem with this is they have a set number of high as well as a set number of low performers."

"HR professionals often concentrate 80 percent of their efforts on 20 percent of employees. The problem is that it is the wrong 20 percent. The focus is typically on employees with issues, complainers, and those who seem to make the most noise. The effort should instead be applied to keeping the best 20 percent of employees happy (i.e., the high performers) in order to ensure the cream of the crop stays satisfied."

"High performers not only exceed expectations but create innovative, new projects that best showcase the company or organization. It means looking beyond your job description and seeing the big picture of success and how you can help get the company or organization there."

"Most organizations do not reward the truly high performers, because too much emphasis is placed on equity and fairness, and also on fitting in, and not enough on what value the individual adds to the organization. I would rather have one high performer than have three meets-expectations types among the people I supervise. Organizational cultures frequently work to bring everyone to the lowest acceptable level, rather than showcasing excellence. We have become a nation of 'everyone should feel good' and 'everyone should get a trophy' instead of recognizing what is truly exceptional performance."

What Sets High Performers Apart

Aside from establishing high-performance criteria, there are other things that set these individuals apart in the organization, such as attitude, ability to prioritize, initiative, and quality of work (see Survey: What Sets Them Apart). Other characteristics that set apart high-performing people are execution, communication skills, and people skills.

Interestingly, the factors that the fewest business leaders cited as setting high performers apart were quantity of work, persuasiveness, efficiency, and innovation. There are also some differences based on company size. Business leaders at large organizations say high-performing individuals are set apart by the ability to prioritize and attitude, followed by initiative, execution, and communication skills. At small companies, high performers are set apart by attitude, initiative, and quality of work. As you'll see later, some of these characteristics perfectly map to certain Executive Skills that are found in high performers in various positions they hold.

SURVEY: WHAT SETS THEM APART

"What would you say sets apart the high-performing individuals in your department and/or organization?"

Attitude	77%
Ability to prioritize	72%
Initiative	68%
Quality of work	67%
Execution	64%
Communication skills	63%

People skills	63%
Adaptability	60%
Attention to detail	42%
Creativity	40%
Productivity	34%
Innovation	33%
Efficiency	32%
Persuasiveness	30%
Quantity of work	18%

Voices from the Front Lines: What Sets Them Apart

"It's all about drive, determination, and desire."

"I find I am more and more seeking people with positive attitudes to join my team. I can do a lot as long as the person is willing and able to learn and grow."

"All high performers are hard working, diligent, and pay attention to detail. People that truly excel are also innovative and creative. There are too few in today's management, however."

"The high-performing individuals in my organization are able to generate repeat business through customers who specifically request them on projects."

"If I had to choose, attitude and adaptability would be my first choices across the board."

"High-performing individuals just 'go for it.' They are willing to tackle a problem, project, or challenge, and don't hesitate."

"Attitude, attitude, attitude. It will overcome all of the other limitations."

"The highest performers in our organization routinely challenge 'the way we've always done things,' creating better processes, improving communication, and, in the end, delivering better value to our customers."

"I would add a high tolerance for ambiguity, especially in our fast-changing environment."

"Highly productive people do whatever it takes to get the job done right. They are also more results-oriented in contrast to just action-oriented."

"High-performance characteristics differ by job. When you've got the right person in the right job, you've got a high performer."

"Regardless of how cynical this may sound, one person may be high-performing with one supervisor and not high-achieving in another situation. Although there are individuals who perform well in most all situations, they are rare."

It could be that attitude, or at least positive attitude, may be exhibited in high performers as a whole because their Executive Skills strengths are a good match for the positions they hold and tasks with which they are charged. This could make them seem more positive toward their work, since that work is more natural for them because their Executive Skills strengths are a good match for the tasks at hand. And ability to prioritize could also be compared to the Executive Skill of Planning/Prioritization, one of the most frequently found strengths in high performers overall.

As you can see, different organizations have differing approaches to identifying who is a high performer within their organizations, though none have difficulty identifying precisely who they are. In the next chapter, we detail what Executive Skills are found in high performers overall, what combinations of skills typically are found with each other, and what strengths are found in high performers based on the industry in which they work. Then you can begin to match your strengths with the strengths of high performers in various areas.

4

Navigating Your Road to High Performance

Finding Your Skills Combination to Determine What Industry You Should Be In

ONCE YOU KNOW the most commonly found Executive Skills strengths of high performers in a particular industry, you can match your own strengths to those strengths to see what industry might best suit you.

And by knowing the most commonly found strengths in an industry, you can more easily spot them and devise ways to more effectively interact with people with those strengths. Even more importantly, the same is true for identifying common Executive Skills weaknesses and then understanding which of your own strengths and weaknesses are the same or different, which can help you determine better ways to interact.

When it comes to Executive Skills, there aren't some that are good and some that are bad. However, there are certain of these skills that are more frequently found in certain parts of work than in others. Significant percentages of high performers in various jobs, departments, and industries possess similar Executive Skills strengths. There also are Executive Skills that go hand in hand, so if you identify one in a person, there's a good chance the person has a particular other one. The same is true for opposites, so if a person is strong in one skill, he or she is likely weak in a certain other one, as you'll see.

Once you know this, you can watch for patterns both in yourself and in others. For example, if you identify that a high performer seems to be very flexible, that same person is likely not to be highly organized. The key, however, is to identify and match your strengths to those of high performers and then go from there.

Most Prevalent Executive Skills Strengths and Weaknesses

The three most frequently found strengths across all high performers in business are Working Memory, Planning/Prioritization, and Organization. The characteristics that go along with these strengths are having the ability to do one task without losing sight of other commitments or obligations, being reliable, being able to keep your eye on the ball, and being likely to follow through. These high performers tend to keep track of belongings and pay attention to detail; are clear-thinking, with an aptitude to develop step-by-step processes; and are able to differentiate what's important and what's not. At the bottom of the list of commonly found strengths are Time Management, Task Initiation, and Sustained Attention, which means that a relatively small percentage of high performers possess these skills as a strength.

These three Executive Skills in the high performers as a group are not each mutually exclusive as a strength. For example, of those strong in Working Memory, almost all are either strong or not weak in Planning/Prioritization. And of those strong in Planning/Prioritization, a significant number are either strong or not weak in Working Memory. This pattern is similar across all most frequently found skills.

When it comes to the weakest skills of high performers, the most frequently found are Task Initiation, Emotional Control, and Stress Tolerance. Interestingly, two of the three strengths of high performers (Working Memory and Planning/Prioritization) are at the bottom of the list of weaknesses, meaning that the overall strengths of high performers are consistent with the weaknesses at the other end of the spectrum. The characteristics of the weaknesses are a tendency to procrastinate before starting projects, to be emotional and sensitive to criticism, to be resistant to change, and to be uncomfortable with uncertainty.

So if you also are weak in, say, Task Initiation, you know that you tend to put things off, a common trait of high-performing individuals in business. That doesn't mean that things you have to do don't get finished on time, but they're not typically going to get started right away.

The Executive Skill that rates as the most significant across high performers overall is Planning/Prioritization. This skill is what we call the *Differentiator,* with 91 percent of high performers not weak in it and it being among the leading strengths.

Again, there are exceptions to the rule, so if you're weak in Planning/Prioritization, you still could be a high performer. However, with about nine out of ten high performers not weak in it, the chances are significantly smaller than for someone who has it as a strength. And if you or someone you're about to promote is strong in Planning/Prioritization, all other things being equal, that person has a much higher likelihood of being a high performer.

Executive Skills Strengths: Overall High Performers

Working Memory

Planning/Prioritization

Organization

Executive Skills Weaknesses: Overall High Performers

Task Initiation

Emotional Control

Stress Tolerance

Differentiator: Overall High Performers

Planning/Prioritization

There were several Executive Skills not among the leading three strengths and weaknesses of high performers. While these skills don't seem to be a factor for high performers overall, they do come into play in more specific breakdowns, such as by job function or title, which we discuss later.

Some Skills Go Hand in Hand

Certain Executive Skills strengths go naturally with each other, and now we know which are commonly paired in high performers. In some cases, high performers strong in a particular skill are strong in another Executive Skill, and vice versa. For example, those strong in Flexibility are also strong in Stress Tolerance and those strong in Stress Tolerance are also strong in Flexibility. So if you are a high performer strong in Flexibility, there's a high probability that you're also strong in Stress Tolerance.

There's an interesting aspect in some of the other combinations. If high performers are strong in one Executive Skill and many of them also are strong in a second skill, the opposite is not necessarily true. For example, those strong in Working Memory are also strong in Organization and Planning/Prioritization. Only a small percentage of them are strong in Sustained Attention.

However, looking at them the other way, of those strong in Sustained Attention, the other leading skill they also are strong in is Working Memory. Likewise, of those strong in Task Initiation, the other skills they are strong in are Organization and Working Memory, but a relatively small percentage of those strong in Organization or Working Memory are also strong in Task Initiation.

You can check your own strengths (see the Commonly Shared Executive Skills Strengths table) to see the likely matching Executive Skills if you're considered to be a high performer.

Many of the common pairings also would seem to be logical combinations in an individual. For example, if you're strong in Metacognition, you would naturally keep reexamining how to better do something. You'd have to be flexible enough to be able to actually change how something is done as a way to improve it. And for those high performers strong in Metacognition, sure enough, one of the other shared strengths they have is Flexibility.

If you're strong in Time Management, you'd find it easy and natural to figure how long it takes to complete a project at work. You're also likely to be very good at keeping order around you. It turns out that a common shared strength in high performers strong in Time Management is Organization, a very logical fit.

High performers strong in Emotional Control can easily keep their cool under the gun and not be overly bothered by it. They also are not likely to go off on a rant or rave when something gets out of hand, but rather take it calmly without getting upset. Again, there is a logical pairing of skills of high performers strong in Emotional Control, as they are also strong in Response Inhibition, which means they very naturally tend to think before they speak, even when they might be upset.

Another advantage of knowing which skills typically go hand in hand with others is seeing it in those you may manage. For example, if you're a manager and one of your high-performing employees is obviously strong in Goal-Directed Persistence, that person also is likely to be good at improvement along the way to completion of a long-term project (strong Metacognition), likely to sequence events of the project very logically (strong Planning/Prioritization), or likely not to let things fall through the cracks along the way (strong Working Memory).

And if a person is very good at managing time, that person is also likely to be highly organized (strong Organization) or good at knowing which items to tackle first (strong Planning/Prioritization).

COMMONLY SHARED EXECUTIVE SKILLS STRENGTHS

EXECUTIVE SKILLS STRENGTH	ADDITIONAL STRENGTHS
Response Inhibition	Emotional Control, Metacognition
Working Memory	Organization, Planning/Prioritization
Emotional Control	Response Inhibition, Flexibility
Sustained Attention	Working Memory, Planning/Prioritization
Task Initiation	Organization, Working Memory
Planning/Prioritization	Organization, Working Memory

Organization	Planning/Prioritization, Working Memory
Time Management	Organization, Planning/Prioritization
Goal-Directed Persistence	Metacognition, Planning/Prioritization, Working Memory
Flexibility	Metacognition, Stress Tolerance
Metacognition	Goal-Directed Persistence, Flexibility
Stress Tolerance	Flexibility, Metacognition

Strengths vs. Commonly Found Weaknesses

In addition to spotting which of your strengths or the strengths of others match certain other strengths, there are typical matches of strengths with weaknesses. Identifying these also can help you determine in advance how to more effectively interact with others.

The opposite strengths and weaknesses can be one way but not the other. For example, high performers strong in Flexibility are weak in Task Initiation, but a majority of those strong in Task Initiation are weak in Emotional Control, with significantly fewer weak in Flexibility.

In other cases, the corresponding strengths and weaknesses are the same. For example, the most frequently found weakness of high performers strong in Emotional Control is Task Initiation, and the most commonly found weakness of those strong in Task Initiation is Emotional Control.

This information could be useful if you don't know the entire Executive Skills profile of someone but you're considering involving him or her in a team project. While you may not know each of the person's 12 strengths and weaknesses, you may recognize some of the more obvious of them and use the Executive Skills Strengths with Corresponding Weaknesses table as a guide.

For example, if a person is always very adaptable when asked to modify or change something, that person may be strong in Flexibility. If the individual is a high-performing individual, there is a higher probability that he or she also is weak in Task Initiation or Organization, the most commonly found opposites of Flexibility in high performers overall.

As in strengths matches, many of the strength-weakness combinations seem logical. High performers strong in Response Inhibition tend to think before they speak. At times, they can be perceived to be overly thoughtful or analytical. Logically, they may tend to not start a project until they've thought things through. Interestingly, the most frequently found corresponding weakness in those strong in Response Inhibition is Task Initiation, a logical fit with being thoughtful. If you have that combination, you are likely to delay action while you think more about it.

High performers strong in Planning/Prioritization are very natural at coming up with a plan, with all sequences of that plan in order. They may have little patience or tolerance for those who either can't see the logic of it or execute against it. The most commonly found weakness of those strong in Planning/Prioritization is Emotional Control.

EXECUTIVE SKILLS STRENGTHS WITH CORRESPONDING WEAKNESSES

EXECUTIVE SKILLS STRENGTH	LEADING EXECUTIVE SKILLS WEAKNESSES
Response Inhibition	Task Initiation, Stress Tolerance
Working Memory	Emotional Control, Task Initiation
Emotional Control	Task Initiation, Organization
Sustained Attention	Stress Tolerance, Emotional Control
Task Initiation	Emotional Control, Stress Tolerance
Planning/Prioritization	Emotional Control, Task Initiation
Organization	Stress Tolerance, Emotional Control

Time Management	Emotional Control, Stress Tolerance
Goal-Directed Persistence	Task Initiation, Emotional Control
Flexibility	Task Initiation, Organization
Metacognition	Task Initiation, Organization
Stress Tolerance	Task Initiation, Organization

High-Performing Males vs. High-Performing Females

It turns out that high-performing males and females have the same two of the three most frequently found Executive Skills. We aren't aware of any other large-scale research project that measured any Executive Skills differences by gender, certainly not of high-performing individuals in business.

While both male and female high performers are strong in Working Memory and Planning/Prioritization, there's one notable difference: The most frequent Executive Skill in males and females is totally different.

The top strength in the largest number of high-performing males is Metacognition, the ability to stand back and take a bird's-eye view of yourself in a situation and be able to understand and make changes in how you solve problems.

In females, the most common strength is Organization, the ability to arrange according to a system.

In both cases, the most commonly found strength in males vs. females is in the middle of the other's most commonly found strengths, indicating that the respective strengths of males and females are truly unique.

While the most frequently found strengths in male high performers are Metacognition, Planning/Prioritization, and Working Memory, the fewest number of high-performing males are strong in Time Management, Task Initiation, or Sustained Attention.

Interestingly, one of the most commonly found weaknesses in males is Organization, the most commonly found strength in females. The other weaknesses most commonly found in males are Task Initiation and Emotional Control.

So if you're male and can't start things on time, or can't keep track of your belongings, or get upset about things, you could have some of the same weaknesses as high-performing males.

The Differentiator for male high performers is Metacognition, with it being the most commonly found strength and not a weakness for 88 percent of high performers.

If you're a manager and identify a high-performing male, there's a good chance he will be strong in at least one of the three skills identified.

Executive Skills Strengths: High-Performing Males

Metacognition

Planning/Prioritization

Working Memory

Executive Skills Weaknesses: High-Performing Males

Task Initiation

Organization

Emotional Control

Differentiator: High-Performing Males

Metacognition

While the most frequently found strengths in female high performers are Organization, Working Memory, and Planning/Prioritization, the strengths found in the least number of high-performing females are Stress Tolerance, Time Management, and Emotional Control.

Not only are those three skills at the bottom of the most commonly found strengths in females, but two of them are among the most frequently found weaknesses.

So if you're female and know where things go, or remember critical things to do when very busy, or easily decide what you should tackle next, you could have some of the same strengths as high-performing females.

The Differentiator for female high performers is Working Memory, with 88 percent of females not weak in it and it being one of the most frequently found strengths.

Executive Skills Strengths: High-Performing Females

Organization

Working Memory

Planning/Prioritization

Executive Skills Weaknesses: High-Performing Females

Emotional Control

Stress Tolerance

Task Initiation

Differentiator: High-Performing Females

Working Memory

Executive Skills of High Performers by Age

Whether you're in your 20s or your 50s, if you're a high performer, there's not likely to be a difference in your Executive Skills strengths. When we compare those two age ranges of high performers, the most frequently found strengths essentially matched in both groups. We found no discernible differences in Executive Skills strengths based on age.

This seemed logical as well, since Executive Skills strengths are relatively fixed from adulthood on.

Task Initiation: The Common Weakness

You probably know people in business (or in life) who tend to put off starting things (maybe even you do this). You know they mean well. They get an assignment on Tuesday and are told it's due in exactly two weeks. They decide to think about the assignment on Wednesday; after all, Tuesday is almost over. On Wednesday, they decide to tackle it at the end of the day, at which time they conclude it's too late in the day to start it. The next day, they figure it's too late in the week to start it, so they put it off until Monday, when they know they'll be fresh. Monday rolls around and they decide that since they have all week there's no need to start it today. Next time it gets considered to start is Wednesday, but other things have to get done first. Well, there's always tomorrow, Thursday. Oh, they forgot that they have to start that other project that was put off a few weeks back. That one is due Friday, the next day. Then they'll have a clear deck to start this project. Friday comes around, and it takes all day to complete the first project. Then there are weekend commitments, so the plan is to start it on Monday. This entire process takes exactly one day less than two weeks, which is perfect, because it isn't due until Tuesday, which is the next day.

The previous paragraph describes precisely what behaviors of someone low in the Executive Skill of Task Initiation might look like. If you're weak in Task Initiation, it might be something like how you act. The person could plan to start something right away, but it just never seems to happen. It's not an example of bad intentions, just a certain Executive Skills weakness.

Someone could easily argue that to get something done at work it needs to get started first. Some might even argue that it needs to get started right away. While many businesspeople may think that getting things started quickly is important for high performers, our study indicates quite the opposite.

Across all high-performing individuals, Task Initiation is the most commonly found Executive Skills weakness, identified in 43 percent of high performers (88 percent did not have it as a strength). Almost half of CEOs are weak in Task Initiation, and more than half of those with the title of chairman, owner, or partner are weak in the skill. More males than females are weak in it. So if you don't tend to naturally start things right way, you're not alone.

Even though high performers are weak in Task Initiation, it doesn't mean some things don't get started when they need to, for several potential reasons.

1. *Aids or Cues.* Even though a high performer is weak in Task Initiation, external factors could cause the person to start something right away. For example, an executive assistant can keep an executive running on time throughout the day. The assistant can help control scheduling, interrupt when one meeting needs to end so that another can start, and deflect issues that could disrupt schedules from a time standpoint. The high performer also may be in an environment where someone is telling him or her to start something because that person needs it right away, leaving no choice for delay.

2. *External Factors.* The main projects and tasks on the table may only be the absolutely critical tasks at the moment. So while many tasks are not being started on time, the absolutely critical ones are moving forward rapidly because they dominate the agenda of the moment. A person low in Task Initiation may expect to put off a particular task on a given day but be forced by circumstances to tackle it because it becomes the crisis of the moment, not a rarity in business today. This is also partly an external factor—that is, out of the control of the high performer.

3. *Compensating Executive Skills.* While a high performer may be weak in Task Initiation, he also could be strong in Goal-Directed Persistence. So while his brain puts off starting something right away, it conveniently calculates the last possible minute to start that project in order to get it done on time. While starting the task is not considered to be critical (weak Task Initiation), completing it by the deadline is paramount (Goal-Directed Persistence). This combination can quite easily annoy a person with the opposite Executive Skills combination, since she would only consider starting the task right away but may lose sight of the end goal. She also could be annoyed because she doesn't comprehend how the high performer never starts the critical quarterly reports when he should but always gets them in on time.

So the next time you see that someone you assign a task to doesn't start it right away, there may be no need to panic. It may be that the person does not start the assignment immediately but ultimately will deliver when it is required to be finished.

The High-Performing Pair

In some cases, high performers may be that way because over time they instinctively figured out what they were lacking and found a way to have someone else compensate for their weakness to create an even stronger combination.

SCENARIO:
Paige is a clinical technician at a well-known regional hospital. She's highly organized and is a fast starter at everything she does. She likes things the way they are, with everything in its proper place, which

she always makes sure of before she leaves work every day. It used to really bother her when she'd come back the next day and find that the person on the previous shift scattered the instruments randomly. She can't understand why others can't put things back exactly where they go. She used to get upset about these kinds of things until she started working with Anthony last year. They've been a two-person clinical team ever since. Before Anthony teamed with Paige, he was the ultimate procrastinator. He was so easily sidetracked from starting any task at hand. Something would come along that caught his attention and he'd divert right to that. He'd get lectured by the director of the department about being late starting even though she praised him for always being willing to drop what he's doing to help someone else.

Since the two started working together, Paige has taken responsibility to get things going and keep them on schedule. She organizes the team's day. This is easy for her because she's strong in Task Initiation and Organization. When things change, as they always do, rather than get upset, Anthony helps Paige to relax, telling her there's nothing to worry about, and Anthony jumps in to plot the lead on the new direction. That's natural for Anthony because he's strong in Flexibility and Emotional Control. Anthony covers for Paige's weaknesses (Emotional Control, Stress Tolerance), and Paige covers for Anthony's (Task Initiation). More significantly, together they have the strengths of Task Initiation, Organization, Emotional Control, and Flexibility. Together, Paige and Anthony are the ultimate high-performing couple.

It's possible that in the case of many high performers, they've devised or fallen into mutually beneficial Executive Skills situations where two people actually make up a high performer or at least explain the reasons for the high performance. One person may be strong in Organization and Planning/Prioritization and the other in Task Initiation and Working Memory. Together, they can be a strong combination, with the pair starting projects right away, creating a logical road map with a high degree of organization, and are not likely to let anything fall through the cracks. The combined strengths of the two people are far greater than the strengths of either of the individuals.

Some might also suggest that compatible couples frequently possess complementary Executive Skills, which adds to a smoother relationship. For example, a husband may be strong in Goal-Directed Persistence while the wife is strong in Task Initiation. He may promise to clean the garage by the beginning of spring, a target he would surely hit, but she would be more likely to get him to start a month sooner than he would have, making completion a lot easier than doing it all at the last minute, which is what he would have done. Conversely, a wife may be weak in Organization, and as a result she misplaces her car keys on a regular basis, while the husband is strong in it and always very naturally knows where to look to find them.

So on your road to high performance, you may want to partner with someone with complementing strengths at certain times and in certain situations. And if you manage others, you can look to do the same, perhaps naming a two-person team with different and complementing strengths to tackle a major project.

Executive Skills of High Performers by Industry

High performers share similar Executive Skills based on industry, as well as other categories that we explain later. High performers in financial services, healthcare, manufacturing, technology, education, and nonprofits have some of the same Executive Skills strengths in some cases but in others they are totally different. Across the six industries, there's not one strength among the three most frequently found in all industries. However, there are several strengths not among the three most common in *any* of the industries.

We queried people with a range of titles, from employee, manager, and director to CEO, owner, and partner, in a variety of departments, including accounting, customer service, finance, marketing, operations, and sales.

One of the benefits of knowing the strengths and weaknesses of high performers by industry is that it may make it easier for you to identify a potentially new industry you may not have previously considered.

Once you see the common strengths of high performers by industry, you can compare your strengths to see where there's a match. In some cases, at least one of your strengths may match more than one industry. This means you have a high probability of becoming a high performer in those industries, all other things being equal. And if your strengths match the strengths of high performers in a particular industry, it means those high performers will essentially see things at work the same way as you.

Even if you don't change industries, knowing the likely strengths of the high performers by industry can provide insight into how you might understand how to better interact with people in those industries. For example, if you know that a prevalent strength in a particular industry is Metacognition, you can expect that a person you may be trying to market a product or service to may be more open to considering the product, since that person would naturally want to look for ways to improve.

You also can leverage information about common weaknesses of high performers in any given industry. For example, if you know that Task Initiation is a common weakness of high performers in an industry, you may need to take it upon yourself to take the initiative to get things going. If you know that Emotional Control is a common weakness, you may want to be more careful about choosing your words; otherwise, the person you are dealing with may become upset, even though he or she may not show it at the time.

If the person you're dealing with is weak in Organization, you can take it upon yourself to make sure all the necessary paperwork or information is prepared in advance of a meeting, since that person is likely to misplace it.

You also should compare your strengths and weaknesses to those of the high performers in the industry before interactions. If you have the same strengths, you're likely to approach issues the same way. Where the skills differ, you can plan in advance how to compensate, so that the person with the particular strength takes the lead on issues that call for that strength.

If the person in an industry is strong in Time Management and that is one of your weaknesses, you should allow the other person to control the timing and pacing of the meeting as well as have more significant input as to how long it may take to do something. The other person would have a much higher probability of estimating accurately.

The converse also is true, so if you are strong in Time Management and the other person is weak, you should do the time estimates. You also can expect the other person to be late for the meeting, even though you'll show up on time. In such a case, bring something along to do, such as unrelated paperwork, so that you can be productive while waiting for the person and not become aggravated by her lack of Time Management, since it's natural for you but not for her. It's how she's wired.

Financial Services

Should you be in financial services, which includes financial, real estate, and insurance as categories and comprises well-known large and small banking institutions, insurance companies, credit unions of all sizes, multiple listing services, and investment groups?

The high-performing individuals in financial services are goal-driven, able to observe and correct their own actions, and likely to remember the critical detail at the critical time. This is because the Executive Skills strengths most frequently found in these high performers are Metacognition, Goal-Directed Persistence, or Working Memory.

So if you're strong in Metacognition, you likely also are strong in Goal-Directed Persistence. If you're strong in only one of these skills, there's still a higher probability that you could be a high performer in financial services than someone who doesn't have that same strength.

This also doesn't mean that if you share one or more of the Executive Skills strengths of high performers here that you should work in financial services, just that the way your brain is wired would make it more natural for you to become a high performer there. But as you will see, this would not be your only option of fit, since some of the same strengths are leading strengths in other industries as well.

The most frequently found weaknesses in financial services are Task Initiation, Emotional Control, and Organization. With more than 40 percent of high performers weak in Task Initiation, you can expect that some things get put off. However, with the counterbalance of strong Goal-Directed Persistence, starting late likely may not cause any significant issues.

Some Executive Skills don't seem to play a significant role in high performers in financial services. For example, roughly the same number of high performers are strong as are weak in Organization. Time Management is another one, since only about one in ten high performers is strong in it, while almost a third are weak in it. Those Executive Skills that are not the most frequently found are less likely to be of significance in any given category.

More than a third of high performers in financial services are strong in Metacognition, and relatively few count it as a weakness, making it the Differentiator in that industry. So if that is your leading strength, there's a good chance you could be a high performer in financial services, if you so chose.

Executive Skills Strengths: Financial Services

Metacognition

Goal-Directed Persistence

Working Memory

Executive Skills Weaknesses: Financial Services

Task Initiation

Emotional Control

Organization

Differentiator: Financial Services

Metacognition

Healthcare

If you're highly methodical, perhaps you could be a high performer in healthcare. High performers in healthcare, which includes medical and dental, work in large and small hospitals, medical laboratories, therapy organizations, and various types of medical centers, are in departments including administrative, clinical, general management, human resources, marketing, sales, and information technology and hold a wide range of titles, including CEO, vice president, director, manager, and employee.

Besides being considered to be methodical, they are likely to be great at drawing on past experience to deal with problems, may have well-developed systems for tracking information, or be able to quickly determine what's important and worth dealing with and what is not.

This is because the most frequently found Executive Skills in these high performers are Working Memory, Organization, or Planning/Prioritization. Interestingly, the strengths found most frequently in high performers in healthcare are identical to the three most frequently found skills in the population of high performers as a whole.

Now this is not to suggest that everyone who works in healthcare will be strong in one or more of these Executive Skills, since it depends on what area of healthcare it is. For example, as you'll see later, high performers in clinical areas have different Executive Skills strengths than those who work in a business office within the healthcare industry.

So if you're getting medical treatment, the interactions with the office or administrative staff may be different from those with the medical professionals treating you, and those interactions are partly because of how those people's brains are wired. Perhaps more significantly, if you work in a clinical area and are looking to move to the business office, for whatever reason, it could be helpful to know that the most frequently found strength of those in clinical is different from the one most frequently found in high performers on the business side, since you may or may not have that as a strength.

However, there are a number of high performers in clinical departments who possess that particular Executive Skills strength; it's just a matter of identifying if you have it before the execution of a transfer or promotion that has a high probability of success or failure based on an Executive Skills match or mismatch.

The Executive Skill that can make the difference in high performers in healthcare is Planning/Prioritization, the Differentiator, with 91 percent of high performers *not* low in it and it ranking among the three most frequently found strengths. If you're strong in Planning/Prioritization, you have a higher probability of becoming a high performer in healthcare than someone who is not.

Executive Skills Strengths: Healthcare

Working Memory

Organization

Planning/Prioritization

Executive Skills Weaknesses: Healthcare

Stress Tolerance

Emotional Control

Task Initiation

Differentiator: Healthcare

Planning/Prioritization

Manufacturing

If you're continually observing how you solve problems and looking for ways to improve, both personally and for those you work with, maybe manufacturing is for you.

High performers in manufacturing are in a range of departments, from accounting and research and development to general management and operations, with titles including CEO, CFO, COO, director, manager, and employee.

They easily see what needs to be dealt with and when and are naturally good at establishing systems to get things done. These characteristics may seem obvious as they would be useful in manufacturing, where continual improvement and effective operational systems are key. And those characteristics are most frequently found in high performers there, with the most frequently found skills to be Metacognition, Planning/Prioritization, and Organization, which could help explain why they're considered high performers in their organizations.

However, even though Organization is a commonly found strength in manufacturing high performers, it's not a critical or differentiating skill, since about the same percentage of high performers have it as a weakness. Interestingly, a large number of the high performers weak in Organization are strong in Emotional Control, which would allow them to more easily manage emotions to reach their goals. You may recall that Emotional Control and Organization are typical opposite Executive Skills, so if you're a high performer strong in one, you're likely to be weak in the other.

In addition to Organization, the other weaknesses most often found in manufacturing high performers are Task Initiation or Time Management.

The Differentiator for high performers in manufacturing is Metacognition, with 91 percent of high performers not low in it and it being the most frequently found strength. So if you're strong in Metacognition, your chances of being a high performer in manufacturing are high, as they are for finance, as you may recall.

Executive Skills Strengths: Manufacturing

Metacognition

Planning/Prioritization

Organization

Executive Skills Weaknesses: Manufacturing

Task Initiation

Time Management

Organization

Differentiator: Manufacturing

Metacognition

Technology

If one of your leading strengths is Planning/Prioritization, technology could be your arena. High performers in the technology industry came from all departments, including sales, research and development, information technology, operations, marketing, general management, and legal, with titles that range all the way from CEO to employee. Companies include the best-known computer makers, as well as global and regional hardware and software companies.

In high performers in technology companies, there's a clear distinction between strengths and weaknesses. The most frequently found strength is Planning/Prioritization, while a majority of high performers are weak in Task Initiation. So high performers are likely to be methodical in how they approach things, very naturally creating sequences of what goes before what, but not starting right away.

As you'll see later, Planning/Prioritization is a key strength not only in technology companies, but in people who work in information technology as well. At some companies in the study, large majorities of high performers in IT departments are strong in Planning/Prioritization.

For high performers in technology, as in manufacturing, Organization is equally a strength and a weakness, negating its significance. Working Memory is the other leading strength and Time Management the other weakness, both found in about a third of high performers.

The Differentiator is Planning/Prioritization, it being the most frequently found strength and not a weakness in 91 percent of high performers. If you're strong in Planning/Prioritization, technology companies could be a natural fit for you to become a high performer, as well as healthcare or manufacturing.

Executive Skills Strengths: Technology

Planning/Prioritization

Working Memory

Organization

Executive Skills Weaknesses: Technology

Task Initiation

Emotional Control

Time Management

Differentiator: Technology

Planning/Prioritization

Education

High performers in education, which includes educational services, are from universities, colleges, and high schools, both public and private. Titles include CEO, principal, director, and employee, and departments include administrative, finance, marketing, operations, education, and public relations.

If you're like them, you're good at self-monitoring and improving how you solve problems, since Metacognition is the most frequently found strength. This would make it very natural for them to continually look for ways to improve the way they and those around them do things.

They're also likely to create road maps or logical plans of how they expect to move ahead and tend to keep track of things they manage. This is because the other most common strengths of these high performers are Planning/Prioritization and Organization.

This could be a good thing, since half of the high performers in education are weak in Task Initiation, followed by Time Management. These weaknesses may not be a problem for high performers in education, since many of the aspects of managing time are self-regulated. For example, in lower schools, bells ring to signal class beginning and ending. The day starts at a specific time and ends at a specific time, and students will let any teacher know if he or she is running over. In upper grades, including college, students don't hesitate to let the teacher know when class is over by packing their belongings or getting up to leave. Environmental factors such as these could make Task Initiation and Time Management much less of a requirement to be a high performer in education.

The other weakness most frequently found in education is Stress Tolerance. This isn't surprising, since someone strong in Organization would likely find it stressful when things become uncertain, which could be unnerving to someone more comfortable with order. Stress Tolerance is also a commonly found weakness in high performers strong in Organization.

The Differentiator in education is Metacognition, with it being the most frequently found strength and not a weakness in 92 percent of high performers. So if you're strong in Metacognition, you now can add education to financial services and manufacturing as areas where the leading skill of high performers matches yours.

Executive Skills Strengths: Education

Metacognition

Planning/Prioritization

Organization

Executive Skills Weaknesses: Education

Task Initiation

Time Management

Stress Tolerance

Differentiator: Education

Metacognition

Nonprofits

In countless conversations with executives and managers in companies of all types, we've heard many times over the years that for-profit organizations are different from nonprofits. To be sure, there are considerable differences, from shareholder demands to accounting regulations. However, when it comes to Executive Skills strengths of high performers who work at for-profit companies compared to those at nonprofits, they're the same.[1]

This means that if you have any of the same strengths as high performers in for-profit organizations, you're just as likely to be a high performer in a nonprofit. This could be good news for you if you've been downsized from a large organization, as you will know that moving to the nonprofit world, some of which is still relatively well-funded, could be easier than you might have thought.

High performers in nonprofits include a wide range of entities, including charities, social services, foundations, neighborhood centers, children's services, care centers, and various types of societies. Most of the nonprofits are relatively small, generally with fewer than 500 employees each, though departments mirror other organizations, such as administrative, general management, accounting, marketing, and sales.

High performers at nonprofits are likely to stay focused on long-term goals and objectives and understand the steps to get there, and are not likely to have things fall through the cracks. The most frequently found Executive Skills strengths in nonprofits are Working Memory, Goal-Directed Persistence, and Planning/Prioritization. If you are strong in Working Memory, you match the strengths of many in nonprofits, as well as those in healthcare, finance, and technology.

High performers at nonprofits are likely to delay starting projects, feel stressed in a crisis, and misplace paperwork when under pressure. This is because the most commonly found weaknesses are Task Initiation, Stress Tolerance, and Organization. Of the six industries, this is the only one where Sustained Attention came close to being a common weakness. So if

Sustained Attention is one of your main weaknesses, it is not likely to be an issue for you working at a nonprofit.

The Differentiator for high performers in nonprofits is Working Memory, with it being the most frequently found strength and relatively few counting it as a weakness.[2] So if you're strong in Working Memory, that skill could be the key for success at a nonprofit, though it's also one of the most common strengths in other industries as well, just not the Differentiator.

Executive Skills Strengths: Nonprofits

Working Memory

Goal-Directed Persistence

Planning/Prioritization

Executive Skills Weaknesses: Nonprofits

Task Initiation

Stress Tolerance

Organization

Differentiator: Nonprofits

Working Memory

Finding the Match

No matter which Executive Skills strengths you have, there's a high likelihood you'll have corresponding strengths and corresponding weaknesses. There's nothing inherently good nor bad about possessing any particular strength or weakness. The real benefit is identifying the strengths and matching those to a particular job, task, function, industry, or career. By reviewing the particular Executive Skills strengths found in high performers, you may be better able to match your own set of Executive Skills against those of high performers based on industry or job title. This may help you predict future success, based on matching to the Executive Skills of those already successful in those roles.

Another value of being able to identify Executive Skills strengths and weaknesses and corresponding combinations is in interacting with others.

Inside an organization, it's relatively easy to identify strengths and weaknesses of people you work with by observing their behaviors. You can use the corresponding strengths and corresponding weaknesses charts in this chapter as an assist to figure the likely combinations of others as well. You also can use this knowledge outside your organization when dealing with clients, customers, and vendors.

Just as we did in our study, you can determine the Executive Skills of the high performers in your area, department, or entire organization. The key then is to ensure that as you move into new positions, your Executive Skills are a good match for the new positions, as we discuss in the next chapter.

5

What's the Right Department for You?

The Strengths of High Performers by Department

BESIDES SEEING which industry might best suit you based on the characteristics of high performers, you also can match Executive Skills by department. High performers have different strengths and weaknesses depending on the department they work in, as you'll see in the 10 departments profiled in this chapter.

By comparing your strengths to those of high performers by department, you can see where there are matches, the same process as by industry. If some of your strengths match those of high performers in a particular department, chances are that you could succeed in that department as well, all other things being equal.

And if you manage others, especially at an executive level, by comparing the strengths of high performers in certain departments, you can get a better feel for what strengths to look for in candidates you may be considering moving into that department.

There's also the added benefit of using these insights to devise ways to better interact with high performers to your advantage once you know the Executive Skills strengths and weaknesses they're likely to possess. This can not only help avoid conflict, but also make communications and interactions more effective, once you know what to look for and expect in the behaviors of the other person.

As you'll see, there are similarities in Executive Skills strengths and weaknesses within any given department, providing insight into what departments may best suit you.

Marketing/Advertising/Promotion: Always Getting Better

If it's very natural for you to continually review actions and activities seeking improvements, you may be well suited for marketing, advertising, or promotion departments. High performers there are strong in Metacognition, Working Memory, or Flexibility.[1] Critical tasks would not likely fall through the cracks for those strong in Working Memory, and changing on the fly for a marketing program would easily fall into place for those strong in Flexibility.

As in many cases, these strengths seem logical based on the functions required for the jobs. You might expect that a successful marketer would always be looking for ways to improve and be flexible to change as market needs change. The significance, however, is that these skills are found in large percentages of high performers in marketing departments, making it predictive that if you have those skills, you could have a good chance of also being a high performer in that department, all other things being equal, of course.

If you're not good at starting on time or managing time well, that wouldn't be a problem for you in marketing, since half of high performers there are weak in Task Initiation, making it normal for projects or activities to be put off until necessary. It could be that tasks aren't started by these high performers naturally but that others or external factors cause them to start things when absolutely required. The time to start projects and the time to complete them would also likely be an issue with these high performers, as relatively few of them are strong in Time Management, and almost a third are weak in it. Again, it would not be the high performers in this environment who would likely be responsible for managing time; that task would fall to others.

Interestingly, the two strengths that would be helpful for creatives, Metacognition and Flexibility (as we identified in *SMARTS*), are each found in more than a third of high performers in marketing/advertising/promotion departments.

Many high performers here may face the issue of keeping their emotions in check, since Emotional Control is the second most frequently found weakness.[2] So while a rejected ad campaign or creative proposal may seem to be taken in stride, it could bother many of these high performers for hours, days, or even weeks without you or others knowing.

The Differentiator for high performers in marketing/advertising/promotion is Metacognition. With 88 percent of high performers here not weak in Metacognition and it being the leading strength, it isn't likely someone weak in this Executive Skill would be a high performer in one of those departments. There are, of course, exceptions, but the likelihood is not high. So if Metacognition is a strength of yours, you'd match many high performers in marketing/advertising/promotion, as well as in general management, as you'll see later in this chapter.

Executive Skills Strengths: Marketing/Advertising/Promotion

Metacognition

Working Memory

Flexibility

Executive Skills Weaknesses: Marketing/Advertising/Promotion

Task Initiation

Emotional Control

Organization

Differentiator: Marketing/Advertising/Promotion

Metacognition

This information can help you deal with people in marketing, notably the high performers, by realizing the common strengths and weaknesses of those you might be dealing with. For example, knowing that the high performers tend to be flexible problem solvers and can draw from past experiences would allow you to give them more leeway in solving a complex problem. If those are your weakest skills, you would want to defer to them even more.

Conversely, knowing many are weak in Emotional Control, Organization, or Task Initiation indicates that it could be more useful to be less focused on the starting time of a project rather than how well it is created and executed. Also, the office of the person you deal with in marketing may look like a disaster area due to his weak Organization, but focusing on the strengths could take away that potentially negative aspect.

Understanding weaknesses of others tends to diffuse conflict in advance.

Sales: Not Falling Through the Cracks

If you tend to not let things fall through the cracks when under the gun, maybe you should be in sales. That skill is a common key for high performers in sales departments, since Working Memory is the most commonly found strength in high performers there. Other strengths are Goal-Directed Persistence, Planning/Prioritization, and Flexibility.[3] As you'll see in a later chapter, the strengths differ from sales employee to sales manager to sales executive, which could help explain why a great salesperson may not become a great sales manager.

As was the case with high performers in marketing, a full half of those in sales share the weakness of Task Initiation. Now you know why great salespeople might procrastinate before heading out for that sales call, or why they never get around to starting that sales or expense report, which is likely to remain on the back burner until absolutely required. And if these salespeople are criticized for this or any other reason, many of them may get upset, since Emotional Control is one of the most frequently found weaknesses, though they may not openly show it.

They also may not be able to find some of those reports, since a most frequently found weakness is Organization. This could help explain why their desks look chaotic and papers are strewn everywhere. You may see a strong salesperson scrambling to get ready for a sales call panic because she can't find her car keys. Now you know why.

For high performers in sales, correctly assessing how long it may take to get to a sales call or how long a meeting will last may be difficult, since only one in ten are strong in Time Management and about a third count it as a weakness. This could also be why a sales presentation is not finished on time, primarily because the salesperson grossly underestimated how long it would take. A solution here, of course, is for the salesperson to ask a high Time Management person to estimate how long the proposal will take and use that as a guideline, not what the salesperson thinks. So if you're a high-performing salesperson and you're calling on a client also low in Time Management, both of you are likely to be late for the start of the meeting, and neither will keep track of how long it should last. The good news is that it won't bother either of you.

The Differentiator in sales is Working Memory, with 89 percent of high performers not weak in it and it being the most frequently found strength. If you're strong in Working Memory, you match the key brain characteristic of high performers in sales.

Executive Skills Strengths: Sales
Working Memory
Goal-Directed Persistence
Planning/Prioritization

Executive Skills Weaknesses: Sales
Task Initiation
Emotional Control
Organization

Differentiator: Sales
Working Memory

In dealing with one of these high performers, you may want to consider that they're likely to hit their end objective (strong Goal-Directed Persistence) but are probably going to have issues starting on time or even calculating time well along the way. Just keep in mind, they will get it done. If your strong skills are the weak skills of these high performers, you may have a tough time understanding how these people get the job done, since they are essentially wired differently than you.

Systems/IT: All About Road Maps

If Planning/Prioritization is one of your strengths, you could be a high performer in systems/information technology. High performers there have a natural ability to create road maps of where they want to go and how to get there, since Planning/Prioritization is the most frequently found strength. In fact, almost no high performers in IT are weak in this skill. This was highlighted in several IT departments, where large majorities shared this strength.

IT high performers can tend to be somewhat reflective, since the second most frequently found strength is Metacognition, followed by Working Memory, making it likely that these people don't forget critical things at critical times. This could be a huge help in all areas of IT, from programming to strategic planning.

The most common weaknesses in high performers in IT are Task Initiation, Stress Tolerance, and Time Management. So while these people may be strong in sequencing tasks and events, they can have a tough time getting started or even accurately determining how long it will take to complete a project. Can you count how many IT projects have been delivered on time? Granted, there often are changes in requirements along the way, but it's still not natural for a high performer in IT to accurately determine how long something will take to complete. This isn't to say they don't mean to; it's just that their brain doesn't process or estimate time with a high degree of accuracy.

The Differentiator for high performers in IT is Planning/Prioritization, with 95 percent of high performers not having it as a weakness and it being the most frequently found strength among this group.

Executive Skills Strengths: Systems/IT

Planning/Prioritization

Metacognition

Working Memory

Executive Skills Weaknesses: Systems/IT

Task Initiation

Stress Tolerance

Time Management

Differentiator: Systems/IT

Planning/Prioritization

When dealing with high performers in IT, you may want to let them devise the planning process, since it will be natural for them to determine which items should be in which order. But you also may want to encourage the meetings to occur, since their low Task Initiation and Time Management are not likely to make that very easy for them to do.

You also may want to keep in mind that when things get very busy and hectic, those high performers will be more prone to put things off and become stressed about the situation.

General Management: Goal-Oriented

If your Executive Skills matched well for marketing, chances are you may also be well suited for general management. High performers here are strong in Metacognition, also the most frequently found skill of those in marketing/advertising/promotion, as noted earlier. General management as a department comprises people with titles from CEO to employee and includes industries of all types. High performers also come from a range of organization size, from 100 or fewer employees to 100,000 or more.

The other top strengths of high performers in general management are Planning/Prioritization and Working Memory.

These high performers are also goal-driven, with more than a third strong in Goal-Directed Persistence and 92 percent *not* weak in it. You may recall that Goal-Directed Persistence was also a leading strength of those with C titles (CEO, CFO, etc.), which would make sense since many of the chiefs are within the category of general management.

The most common weaknesses in general management are Task Initiation, Time Management, and Emotional Control. If you're a high performer in general management and are weak in one of these skills, you probably rely on assistants and others to keep you starting and running on time, since you're not likely to excel in those functions.

The Differentiator for high performers in general management is Metacognition, with 91 percent of high performers not weak in it and it being the most frequently found strength. If Metacognition is one of your strengths, you match the strength of high performers in general management as well as several other departments.

Executive Skills Strengths: General Management

Metacognition

Planning/Prioritization

Working Memory

Executive Skills Weaknesses: General Management

Task Initiation

Time Management

Emotional Control

Differentiator: General Management

Metacognition

Dealing with those in general management should be similar to dealing with those in marketing, at least as it relates to allowing the high performer to devise solutions to problems. You'll face the starting and running on time issue with those in general management, since Task Initiation and Time Management are common weaknesses. If either one of these is one of your strengths, you should control as much as possible the time elements of the interactions between the two of you.

Operations: Good on the Fly

If you could be successful in IT, you also may be well suited for operations departments, where execution is king and where planning and the ability to retool on the fly as things change are common characteristics of high performers. The most frequently found strength is Planning/Prioritization, followed by Metacognition and Flexibility.

High performers in operations also may have some organized self-starters around them, since that would complement their weaknesses.

The most frequent weakness in high performers in operations is Task Initiation, identified in nearly half of them. It's interesting that while operations departments may be noted for getting things done, getting them started is not so natural for high performers there. This weakness was followed by Emotional Control and Organization.

If you're strong in Planning/Prioritization, you possess the Differentiator for high performers in operations, where very few count that skill as a weakness, the same as in IT departments.

Executive Skills Strengths: Operations

Planning/Prioritization

Metacognition

Flexibility

Executive Skills Weaknesses: Operations

Task Initiation

Emotional Control

Organization

Differentiator: Operations

Planning/Prioritization

When dealing with high performers in operations, you may want to keep in mind that while they may have logically sequenced a plan or process, it would be very easy for you to get them to modify that plan if there was a better way. Because of their strong Flexibility or Metacognition, changing from what was established would be no big deal.

Customer Service: Strategically Important

If you're highly organized and highly adaptable, you may be a lot like the high performers in customer service departments.

Customer service is the department that business leaders say provides the most strategic competitive advantage.[4] It's also most frequently cited as the department that provides organizations with the most tactical

competitive advantage. After all, every business needs to satisfy its customers' needs first and foremost, and many business leaders apparently
recognize the importance of those on the front lines.

This leads to the obvious question of which Executive Skills strengths
would be most valuable or are most frequently found in those who are successful in customer service departments. You've probably had both positive
and negative experience with customer service departments. You may have
dealt with customer service reps, whether over the phone or in person, and
found some to seem very together and able to adapt to your needs and others not. The Executive Skills strengths of high-performing people who
work in customer service might help explain why.

The strength most frequently found in high performers in customer
service is Organization, which would make it likely they have an orderly
system to handle problems. Many also are open to new ways to solve customer problems, since they're strong in Flexibility, making them more
likely to be creative and adaptive in problem situations. The third most
commonly found strength is Planning/Prioritization, making it likely that
the customer service person will figure out the sequence of events to solve
a customer's complex problem.

When it comes to weaknesses of high performers in customer service,
the most frequently found are Stress Tolerance, Task Initiation, and Time
Management. These people could feel bad if a customer interaction didn't
go as well as planned. They may seem rushed during a busy day, since they
didn't start something when they should have, leading to a sense of
urgency, and crunched near the end of the day, because things took longer
than expected.

These weaknesses don't appear to be impediments to success in customer service, since they're shared by the high performers. Some of these
weaknesses could be negated by some of their strengths that can compensate for the weaknesses.

For example, a customer service representative may feel bad about an
interaction with a customer (weak Stress Tolerance), but the reaction could
come after the interaction and after the customer is gone. Because the customer service rep likely was prepared for the client or customer interaction
(strong Organization), the result may have been as good as it could be. In

addition, issues could have been outside of the customer service rep's hands, such as a case where a customer is trying to get a difficult issue resolved that's outside the representative's area of responsibility. While a rep may lose track of time during the day and fall behind (low Time Management), he or she is likely to remember to deal with that last pressing issue before leaving (high Working Memory).[5]

The Differentiator for customer service departments is Flexibility, with more than four-fifths of high performers not low in it and it being among the most commonly found strengths. If you're strong in Flexibility, one of your skills matches the key skill of high performers in customer service, so that could be a department for you.

Executive Skills Strengths: Customer Service

Organization

Flexibility

Planning/Prioritization

Executive Skills Weaknesses: Customer Service

Stress Tolerance

Task Initiation

Time Management

Differentiator: Customer Service

Flexibility

In dealing with strong customer service people, it may be helpful to consider that time isn't much under their control, whether starting, tracking, or stopping, such as with a meeting. That means if you're meeting with a high performer in customer service, you should make sure you're the one who gets the meeting started and ended on time—that is, unless those are your weaknesses as well.

Administrative: Organized and Can Adapt

You might expect that high performers who work in administrative departments would require Executive Skills that would allow them to be highly organized, very adaptive, and able to keep things from being missed at the height of chaos, and it turns out that is just the case. The strengths most often found in high performers in administrative departments are Organization, Flexibility, and Working Memory.

And it's a good thing that these high performers are organized and can remember important things when they count, because when things go badly, any of them may get upset, since their top weaknesses are Stress Tolerance and Emotional Control. They're also likely to wait before starting, since many are weak in Task Initiation.

The Differentiator for high performers in administration is Working Memory, so if that is one of your strengths, you're a match for high performers there, as well as in the next department.

Executive Skills Strengths: Administrative

Organization

Flexibility

Working Memory

Executive Skills Weaknesses: Administrative

Stress Tolerance

Emotional Control

Task Initiation

Differentiator: Administrative

Working Memory

When dealing with high performers working in administrative departments, you may want to be somewhat on the delicate side, due to the weaknesses of Stress Tolerance and Emotional Control. However, the people you're dealing with will likely be highly organized, with a good handle on facts based on past activities. And dealing with those strong in Flexibility will allow you to make alternative suggestions that can be considered. You may want to make sure those suggestions are logical and orderly, which would be much easier received by these high performers.

Finance: Modify on the Fly

If you now work in finance and used to work in administrative, or vice versa, your strengths would match those of high performers in either department, since they're the same for both departments.

Finance high performers are likely to be orderly and organized, have a good penchant to recall numbers and data when needed, and be able to modify on the fly based on the changing needs of those they work with. This is because they're strong in Working Memory, Organization, and Flexibility. As in the other department, those in finance hold a wide range of titles, from employee to chief financial officer, and work in a wide range of industries, from nonprofits to financial services businesses.

While many high performers in finance seem highly organized, there are actually more who are disorganized. While Organization is the second most frequently found strength, it's also the second most frequently found weakness. This means that being either strong or weak in Organization is not likely to be a factor to be a high performer in a finance department.

However, these high performers are not likely to get started on their own, since almost half of them are weak in Task Initiation. Many of them also may become upset by something that's said to them in the course of a presentation, since Emotional Control is a weakness in more than a third of them.

In finance, the Differentiator is Working Memory, it being the most commonly found strength in high performers and not a weakness in most of them. If you're strong in Working Memory, you have the Differentiator for finance, administrative, and sales departments.

Executive Skills Strengths: Finance

Working Memory

Organization

Flexibility

Executive Skills Weaknesses: Finance

Task Initiation

Organization

Emotional Control

Differentiator: Finance

Working Memory

If you deal with these people, keep in mind that some will be highly organized and others not, and you should be able to tell pretty quickly by just observing their office, paperwork, or approach to whatever you're discussing. You may want to take the initiative in most cases, due to their low Task Initiation, to get the ball rolling on projects or even scheduling meetings.

The good news is that under pressure they will likely remember a critical element, even if you don't, so if the two of you are in a rushed meeting, you can rely on them to make sure no critical issues are left behind.

Accounting: Methodical Approach

High performers in accounting are likely to be organized and methodical and tend to take a measured step-by-step approach that they can easily lay out even when very busy. They're somewhat like high performers in finance departments in that they're both strong in Organization and Working Memory. However, they are more likely to be organized across the board, since almost half of them are strong in Organization. Rather than it being a weakness in a large percentage of high performers, as it is in finance, Organization is a weakness in only a small percentage of those in accounting.

However, high performers in accounting may not be attracted to high-pressure situations, since the most frequently found weakness is Stress Tolerance, with more than half of them weak in it. As you might have expected, the next most commonly found weakness is Emotional Control, a typical combination with Stress Tolerance, as discussed earlier. And as with those in finance, high performers in accounting are not likely to be natural self-starters, since a commonly found weakness is Task Initiation.

These Executive Skills strengths and weaknesses in accounting could explain why tax accountants tell you not to worry, that your tax return will ultimately get done (high Organization), and then you're finally told that they'll be filing for an extension to the deadline for you (low Task Initiation). They know they'll get your taxes done (high Planning/Prioritization) but have no sense of urgency or underestimate how long it will take to complete all the returns they're working on (low Time Management is right behind low Task Initiation). For high performers overall who are weak in the skills that accounting high performers are strong in, none work in accounting departments.

These combinations of strengths and weaknesses in accounting don't mean that if you have a different combination you can't succeed in that role, but the chances are much lower than for someone whose strengths match those of the high performers.

The Differentiator in accounting departments is Planning/Prioritization, with 93 percent of high performers not low in it and it being found as a leading strength. If you're strong in Planning/Prioritization, this is yet one more department where high performers share that same cognitive function.

Executive Skills Strengths: Accounting

Organization

Planning/Prioritization

Working Memory

Executive Skills Weaknesses: Accounting

Stress Tolerance

Emotional Control

Task Initiation

Differentiator: Accounting

Planning/Prioritization

In dealing with high performers in accounting, you want to consider that these are people who look at things sequentially. They can appear to seem driven and want to stay with a plan. If you get them to vary from that place of organization and method, they may become stressed and upset, since they're more comfortable with things going as planned.

Clinical: Organized and Starting Right Away

If you're good at keeping track of things and tend to pay attention to detail, you may have some of the same makeup of high performers in clinical departments of healthcare. Many of them are likely to be very good at determining next steps, especially in critical situations, and unlike high performers in other departments, many start things right away without any procrastination.

You may think this sounds logical for a healthcare professional in a clinical department, but this is also the Executive Skills profile of the most commonly found strengths in high performers there. The most common strengths are Organization, Planning/Prioritization, and Task Initiation.

In the overall study, there is a relatively even split between male and female respondents, though in clinical departments there are significantly more females than males. You might reason that this explains why Organization is the most frequently found strength since it's also the most frequently found strength in female high performers overall. However, in clinical departments, Organization is also the most frequently found strength in males, so gender doesn't seem to be a factor.

This is one of the rare departments where Task Initiation is a common strength, since many high performers in other departments possess it as a common weakness. It also makes sense that a high performer practicing in a clinical area would need to deal with patients right away rather than procrastinating. Indeed, starting things right away is a characteristic in clinical high performers. But as with Executive Skills, these high performers did not learn this skill; they were basically born with it.

The leading weakness in high performers in clinical departments is Stress Tolerance, which would likely make these people become emotionally distressed in a crisis situation and be resistant to change. They'd also be more comfortable knowing what to expect every day.

Many high performers in clinical departments are weak in Emotional Control, followed by Goal-Directed Persistence, making them somewhat sensitive to or focused on the short rather than the long term, which also seems logical based on what they do each day. Stress Tolerance and Emotional Control are commonly found together in a high performer, so if you're weak in one, there's a good chance you're weak in the other. If you're a high performer strong in Organization, you have a high chance of being weak in Stress Tolerance and/or Emotional Control, as is the case in clinical high performers. This is also true if you're strong in Sustained Attention or Time Management.

For high performers in clinical departments, the Differentiator is Planning/Prioritization, with 92 percent of high performers not low in it and it being one of the top strengths.

Executive Skills Strengths: Clinical

Organization

Planning/Prioritization

Task Initiation

Executive Skills Weaknesses: Clinical

Stress Tolerance

Emotional Control

Goal-Directed Persistence

Differentiator: Clinical

Planning/Prioritization

When interacting with high performers in clinical departments, you can expect them to be organized and ready to go. Keep in mind that because of the weakness in Goal-Directed Persistence, they may be a lot better at starting something than in following it to completion. In such interactions, it would be helpful to have someone involved who is strong in Goal-Directed Persistence, which would be a strong complement to the strengths of a clinical high performer.

Executive Skills in a Department: Clinical High Performers

It can be helpful to see what strengths and weaknesses look like in a department overall, since you often will be interacting with more than one person in any given department. And if you manage others, this could be even more important as you identify typical combinations of strengths of high performers to see what behaviors you can expect based on those strengths.

Chest PT Services is a New England–based home physical therapy service provider. The therapists at Chest PT Services provide healthcare services for patients with cystic fibrosis (CF), a genetic disease that causes mucus secretions to be thicker than normal, according to John Nadeau, who has been president of the company since its founding 30 years ago.[6]

In the airways of the lungs, the thick mucus can cause infection, and patients require various therapies to remove it, one of the therapies being chest physical therapy. Since this is a daily routine until a cure for CF can be found, the therapists provide their services in the patients' homes, a safer environment than health clinics, where infections are more easily acquired. In 2008, the average life expectancy of a cystic fibrosis patient in the United States was the mid-30s.

At Chest PT Services, there's a somewhat distinct profile of the therapists who work there. For example, two-thirds of them are strong in Organization, the most commonly found strength in high performers in clinical departments. More than half of them are strong in Planning/Prioritization, the second most commonly found Executive Skill strength among clinical high performers.

Interestingly, none of the therapists are strong in Stress Tolerance, and almost all are weak in it (Stress Tolerance is the most frequently found weakness among clinical high performers). Almost half of the high performers at Chest PT Services show Flexibility among their weakest skills, and none show it as a strength. Many of the therapists also are strong in Emotional Control, one of the most commonly found weaknesses in clinical high performers overall. (High performers in any given area, such as clinical, possess one or more of the top Executive Skills strengths, but typically not all three. This means that if you're a high performer in clinical, you're likely to have one or more of the most commonly found strengths, but not all of them.)

So the profile of people at Chest PT Services is one of people who are inclined to be neat and keep track of their belongings and easily arrange their schedules to manage the week's work. They're not easily sidetracked and tend to get the job done. They're very good at clear thinking and have the aptitude to develop step-by-step processes and are able to easily determine what's important and what's not. They prefer jobs where they know exactly what to expect every day. Says Nadeau:

Out in patients' homes in various communities around the state, our therapists are required to work very independently and professionally.

In addition to providing therapy treatments, they must, of course, provide the necessary evaluation and documentation to fulfill requirements of the health insurer and medical care system. Our top-performing therapists were identified as those who continually provide excellent health care to their patients, but also who complete the more mundane but necessary reports and get them back into the office with consistent timeliness and accuracy. They are our "go-to" people when a new case comes in because we know that all tasks will be accomplished like clockwork. Essentially, these are the therapists that have made my job easier and their patients' lives healthier for many years.

The Executive Skills profile of our top performers is right on. Their strong Organization is obvious when completing their administrative duties. But what is surprising is that the survey indicates high Emotional Control along with Planning/Prioritization skills. These may define the special skills needed in the healthcare aspect of their job. Our therapists work with patients who have short life expectancies and who require a very vigorous but repetitive form of physical therapy that helps to add years and improve the quality of life. Not much generally changes from day to day, and the treatment routine varies little. Yet the emotional dynamic of a family with one (or more) members having a shortened life is continually in the background. And occasionally our patients become more ill, and for several weeks require more medical care in an attempt to bring them back to "baseline." At these times the therapist must adapt treatments to the new patient status, and help patients to prioritize their care vs. the total time available, in order to optimize treatment success.

In this homecare scenario, our therapists need to provide emotional support as well as physical therapy in a job that, while very repetitive, attempts to fight a relentless disease process to buy time for our patients. Our therapists most often treat the same patients for many years. Each day the treatment requires a high level of physical effort and time. And while therapists must provide adequate time for each patient, the routine generally allows for very stable daily schedules. To avoid situations where there are too many patients per therapist and thus not enough time for adequate treatment, we have always given our therapists the ability to say "no" to additional patients. That apparently has also allowed them to keep their stress levels low, and may be a key reason why so many therapists have been with us for many years, and indicate that they enjoy their work with us.

From the profile it seems that somehow we have found some of the right therapists and they have found the right job. This also helps us understand why some therapists, while very good clinicians who work wonderfully with their patients, just cannot seem to get their paperwork in on time.

As might be expected, we did find differences in Executive Skills in high performers in healthcare based on whether they worked in clinical vs. non-clinical departments, which we detail in the next chapter.

So as you look around your own organization, you likely can identify patterns of behaviors of people based on their Executive Skills strengths and weaknesses, as in the case of Chest PT Services. You also can use this insight to identify patterns of behaviors in those who work at other organizations you may deal with.

Right-Seating People the First Time

Now that you can identify likely Executive Skills strengths in high performers by the department in which they work, you probably have a better understanding of how these characteristics come into play in the everyday world of work. This knowledge can help you move from department to department, a typical scenario in large companies, as top management seeks to broaden those on the way up by exposing some to varying experiences, perhaps as part of management training.

With this knowledge, you can predict with a degree of certainty in advance of a departmental move where there's likely to be a goodness-of-fit situation and where there's likely to be a misfit, creating a potential series of never-ending effortful tasks for you if you're the one being moved. This can be identified in advance by you or by the executive managing the move, or by both.

This understanding of Executive Skills fit and nonfit can be used for career planning as well, either by you or by executives and managers who plot moves of subordinates as they grow within an organization. There will be times that the right people are in the right seats and times when they are not. But by looking at where high performers are found by industry, title, and department, there's a higher probability of placing the right person in the right seat at the right time without the guesswork. The ideal is to get the right person in the right seat every time, not just sometimes. It is all about first-time right-seating.

The other significant aspect of right-seating people the first time is there's less need to monitor whether the right person is in the right seat, which is known in advance with Executive Skills matching. You now know how to identify strengths and weaknesses of high performance by industry and department. This information also should help you deal with people in those industries and departments by identifying their likely behaviors in advance, giving you new ways to deal with them based on the anticipated behaviors. The next step is to identify what strengths and weaknesses look like based on title, which we do in the next chapter.

This can help you match what job you may be likely to be a high performer in by comparing your strengths to those of high performers with those jobs now. If you manage others, you also can see what characteristics match the titles to use for moving people into those jobs with the same Executive Skills strengths, to increase the probability of success.

6

Do You Have What It Takes to Be in the Corner Suite?

Skills Broken Down by Title

Are You in the Right Job?

SOMETIMES YOU may be in the right industry or department but simply in the wrong position. The goal of finding the right job or role, or what we have labeled *first-time right-seating,* is all about creating a goodness-of-fit situation, where your strengths are the same as those required for the job.

The other side of job matching is when your strengths do *not* match what's needed, or situations that are opposite of goodness-of-fit situations. When the job or task plays to your Executive Skills weaknesses, the task is called an *effortful task.* Though you may be able to do it, it will be considerably more difficult than one that plays to your strengths. For example, if you're weak in Task Initiation, you typically have a hard time getting started on a task or project. It's easier and more natural to procrastinate. If you're strong in this skill, you very naturally start immediately without giving it a thought. Same task, different approach.

Over a period of time, sometimes even over many years, you can end up in exactly the right job. It may be that several people before didn't work out in that position but that this time you're a fit. This trial-and-error approach to career planning and promotion can work out, eventually— or not—but it could not be predetermined or predicted with a high degree of accuracy, or at least not scientifically, until now. That's where Executive Skills could be of help by matching your strengths to those required for the particular job or task.

There's also the issue of being promoted or transferred into a position that requires particular Executive Skills that you don't have, or worse, a position that requires what are among your weakest skills, creating the ultimate effortful task situation. This is somewhat common in business, and we explore it in detail in the next chapter. The point is that an Executive Skills mismatch can make it extremely difficult to succeed doing certain functions and also make it feel like very hard work, which may lead you to seek a different position elsewhere, not necessarily realizing why you so disliked your job.

The good news is that identifying the jobs that high-performing individuals in our study hold could provide some insight as to where you or a subordinate might also become a high performer. All other things being relatively equal (technical skills for the job, knowledge of the industry, background, etc.), Executive Skills make the difference in high-performing success. As we discussed earlier, executives and managers don't consider most around them to be high performers. And high performance can occur at any level, whether employee, manager, or executive. As a result, by identifying Executive Skills of high performers by job, it could make it easier for you to see where you likely could be a high performer based on which of your strengths match. This can help you in career planning or even that next potential promotion or transfer.

If you manage others, this knowledge can help when you are considering hiring and promoting by matching the strengths of candidates to those of high performers in our study who hold those positions now. Recognizing the strengths and weaknesses of high performers by title also can help you determine how to more effectively interact with successful people with those titles.

As we travel the country speaking to businesses about Executive Skills, we're asked countless times to tell them which Executive Skills matter most, to which there's no simple answer. Matter most for what? To succeed? In what job? Now or down the road? A CEO will typically ask us what the top Executive Skills are for managers at various levels. Chairmen will ask us the top skills for a CEO. A sales manager wants to know the top skills for a great salesperson.

You may be wondering the same thing. Which Executive Skills are the best for you to have for you to succeed? Because of the range and depth of this study, you're now more likely to ask "Where should I work?" and our study partly answers that question. We say partly because there are no guarantees in business life, as you know. You've already seen the most commonly found Executive Skills in high performers by industry. We also identified the Executive Skills found most frequently in high performers by department and title as well, so now you can see how your Executive Skills match up against those of high performers based on what job they have.

The Brains in the Corner Office

High-performing executives have many similarities in Executive Skills strengths and weaknesses. Of those with "C" titles (CEO, COO, CFO, CIO, CMO), there are patterns. Almost half of those with a "chief" title are strong in Goal-Directed Persistence. This means they'd be natural at keeping their eye on the long-term ball and stay focused on long-term objectives. They would be very natural at defining and achieving goals. Only one out of ten chiefs is weak in this skill. This skill is not a leading one in any of the titles below the C titles other than the title of director. This could help explain why everyone is not cut out to be a CEO or CFO.

Throughout the study, it was typical that in a group, such as by title or department, when any large number of high performers shared one particular Executive Skills strength, a significantly smaller percentage of that same group counted that skill as a weakness, as was the case here. There are five times more chiefs strong in Goal-Directed Persistence than those who are weak in it.

If Goal-Directed Persistence is one of your strengths, you tend to be driven to end-game results and may be well suited to be a chief.

The second most frequently found skill in C titles is Planning/ Prioritization, and only 5 percent show it as a weak skill. This strength would make them approach issues in an orderly fashion, especially in hectic situations. The next leading strength is Working Memory, in more than a third of chiefs.

When it comes to the weakest Executive Skills of chiefs, about half are weak in Task Initiation, three times more than those strong in it. You may recall that Task Initiation is a leading common weakness of high performers overall.

And if you ever wondered why that top executive is frequently late for meetings or loses track of time, the second most frequently found weakness is Time Management.[2] So now you know one more significant role that executive assistants likely play: keeping the chief on time.

This would likely be the case at home as well, since weak Time Management is weak no matter where it goes. Any couple can generally tell who is strong or weak in Time Management, if one or the other possesses it as a high or low Executive Skill. And sometimes just knowing this can reduce the potential conflicts, with each now knowing the actual reason for always being on time (or always being late). The third most frequently found weakness in chiefs is Emotional Control, so they may get upset with something you say to them, whether they show it or not.[3]

The Differentiator for those with a chief title is Goal-Directed Persistence, which is also the most commonly found strength. When comparing CEOs to CFOs, you might think there would be a difference, with one being focused on corporate strategy and direction while the other keeps an eye on finances and economic indicators. In Executive Skills strengths, that is not the case. The three most commonly found strengths in CEOs (Goal-Directed Persistence, Working Memory, Planning/ Prioritization) are the same three most commonly found in CFOs. Not only is it frequently a strength of CEOs, but it is also not a weakness in 94 percent of them.

It is by far the most commonly found strength in both CEOs and CFOs. But when it comes to being late, the CFOs take a slight lead over CEOs. Not one CFO is strong in Time Management, while one in ten CEOs are. Almost half of CFOs are weak in Time Management, the most commonly found weakness. For CEOs, the majority are weak in Task Initiation. This may not matter, since Goal-Directed Persistence can help compensate for the lack of starting on time.

Executive Skills Strengths: C Titles

Goal-Directed Persistence

Planning/Prioritization

Working Memory

Executive Skills Weaknesses: C Titles

Task Initiation

Time Management

Emotional Control

Differentiator: C Titles

Goal-Directed Persistence

So the next time you're dealing with chiefs, you may want to keep in mind that they are likely focused on an end result or a goal, often long-term. They also are not likely to be focused on getting it started, just getting it finished. You can expect many of these chiefs to be scrambling on the way to a goal, since they underestimated how much time it would take and they started late.

If your strengths are Task Initiation or Time Management, you can be a great asset to one of these chiefs as a complement to their weaknesses by taking on the functions that involve managing time and starting tasks.

The Brains Down the Hall

If you're not as focused on that end objective but you're likely to continue to improve methods and processes as you march toward goals, you may be suited to be executive vice president or senior vice president. Just a short distance from that corner office sit these high performers, who are likely to have some, but not all, of the same characteristics of the chiefs.

Both those with chief titles and executive and senior vice presidents are strong in Planning/Prioritization. However, vice presidents are strong in

Metacognition but not Goal-Directed Persistence. This would allow them to naturally focus on continuous improvement, frequently reflecting on their work and the work of others. They'd be able to determine what's important at the time, no matter how much is on their plate. Five times more vice presidents are strong in Metacognition than are weak in it.

As is common in high performers, the weakest Executive Skill in EVP/SVP titles is Task Initiation, with almost half weak in it, four times the number who are strong in that skill, about the same as the C-title executives.

Unlike the chief executives, the top vice presidents cite among their weakest skills Organization or Response Inhibition. This means the area in which they work is likely to be somewhat disorganized looking or they tend to say things that makes others cringe since they often speak before thinking about what they're about to say.

High performers with executive or senior vice president titles have as the Differentiator skill Metacognition, which almost no vice presidents are weak in.[4] If Metacognition is one of your leading strengths, you have a higher probability of being a high-performing senior or executive vice president. You also have a higher probability of being chairman, owner, or partner, since Metacognition is the most commonly found strength among high performers with those titles.

When dealing with high performers with these titles, you can feel free to suggest new ways of doing things, since they will be receptive to continuous improvement. Having thick skin could also be helpful for you, since they are likely to inadvertently say something that they didn't really mean to. And if you're strong in Organization, you can be a great help in finding an item that the other person misplaced, which can be a common occurrence.

Executive Skills Strengths: EVP/SVP

Planning/Prioritization

Metacognition

Working Memory

Executive Skills Weaknesses: EVP/SVP

Task Initiation

Organization

Response Inhibition

Differentiator: EVP/SVP

Metacognition

The Self-Correcting Directors

Next in line come those with the title of director, as in a marketing director or director level in various departments, who are strong in Working Memory, Goal-Directed Persistence, or Metacognition.[5] The weakest skill, which became a pattern across high performers, was Task Initiation, followed by Time Management and Organization.[6]

So a high performer with a director title would likely be frequently reassessing and reviewing to look for ways to improve, much like many high-performing executive and senior vice presidents. They're also likely to stop anything from falling through the cracks when business is hectic or when they're under deadline. They may not always start on time (weak Task Initiation) but are likely to still get done on time (high Goal-Directed Persistence), especially that big project. They may not know where that document is (low Organization) but they remember what it says (high Working Memory).

Outside of the C titles, this is the only other group where Goal-Directed Persistence is among the top strengths in high performers. This isn't to say that if you're a director, then you should be the next CEO. However, it's reasonable to conclude that many high-performing directors have some of that same, long-term drive found in the brains of some of those in the corner office. It would be easier to find someone strong in Goal-Directed Persistence in directors, since many more of them than those with other titles possess the strength. This doesn't mean you couldn't find the skill in people with other titles, but it's highly more likely you'll find it in a high-performing director. So if you're a director and are strong in Goal-Directed Persistence, there are many with the same brain makeup as you working in the corner office.

Executive Skills Strengths: Director

Working Memory

Goal-Directed Persistence

Metacognition

Executive Skills Weaknesses: Director

Task Initiation

Time Management

Organization

Differentiator: Director

Goal-Directed Persistence

If you're strong in either Task Initiation or Time Management, you could be a big help when dealing with directors. If you could become responsible for starting meetings or keeping them on schedule, it would make life for the director a lot easier, since those would be effortful tasks for them.

The Managers with a Plan

If you're a high-performing manager, chances are you're strong in Planning/Prioritization, which you may recall is also the most frequently found skill in executive and senior vice presidents. More than four times the number of managers are strong in Planning/Prioritization as those weak in it. These managers would likely be comfortable with sorting and planning what to do next, determining who they need to meet with, deciding which projects take priority, and planning schedules for the next week. Many of them would be self-correcting as they go (strong Metacognition) and able to keep things in order (strong Organization) based on changing conditions in the office or the market.

Like their business peers, they're not likely to get started on their own (weak Task Initiation) and may become and stay bothered (low Emotional Control, Stress Tolerance) and even upset about what their direct superior told them in a meeting several hours ago.

You shouldn't be surprised if you see a successful manager become upset or stressed out when things don't go as planned, since almost two times more managers are weak in Emotional Control than those strong in it. Another common weakness is Stress Tolerance, commonly found in those weak in Emotional Control, so it's no surprise that almost two times more managers are weak in Stress Tolerance than those strong in it.

But the key skill for managers remains Planning/Prioritization, which is the Differentiator. If you're strong in Planning/Prioritization, holding a title of manager would be a fit based on the brain characteristics of many high-performing managers.

Executive Skills Strengths: Manager

Planning/Prioritization

Organization

Metacognition

Executive Skills Weaknesses: Manager

Task Initiation

Emotional Control

Stress Tolerance

Differentiator: Manager

Planning/Prioritization

Staying cool and calm when dealing with these managers could be helpful, since they are more easily upset and stressed when things don't go as planned. If you know this is going to be the case, it would be best for you to deliver the bad news along with a potential suggestion.

The Organized Employees

High-performing employees may not yet be in the management ranks but they possess several of the same Executive Skills strengths as those ahead of them up the ladder. The largest percentage of them is strong in Organization followed by Working Memory and Planning/Prioritization. These last two are the same strengths found in the C titles as well as executive and senior vice presidents.

So if you're an employee strong in Working Memory or Planning/Prioritization, you have a good chance of succeeding as a high performer both as an employee and at significantly higher levels in an organization. This can help explain why some employees go far up the ladder and some don't, a match or nonmatch of strengths required for higher-level positions.

Among high-performing managers, directors, executive and senior vice presidents, and C titles, Organization shows up as one of the three most common strengths only in high-performing employees and managers. So if you're an employee strong in Organization, that may help you at the employee level but not be as necessary as you move up the ranks, except, of course, to complement other executives weak in it.

Interestingly, the most frequently found weak Executive Skills in high-performing employees (Stress Tolerance, Emotional Control, Task Initiation) are identical to the three most found in managers. So if you're an employee with one or more of these weaknesses, they're not likely to get in the way of a move to a manager role.

The Differentiator for employees is Planning/Prioritization, the same as for managers, further evidence that a high-performing employee has a high probability of becoming a high-performing manager, since many of the Executive Skills combinations are the same for both.

Executive Skills Strengths: Employee

Organization

Working Memory

Planning/Prioritization

Executive Skills Weaknesses: Employee

Stress Tolerance

Emotional Control

Task Initiation

Differentiator: Employee

Planning/Prioritization

Two tables in Appendix B under "Employees vs. Managers vs. Executives" compare the Executive Skills strengths and weaknesses of high performers as employees, managers, directors, executive and senior vice presidents, and C titles.

7

How Your Strengths Match Those of Others at Work

Ways to Match Behaviors to Executive Skills in Your Business

ONCE YOU IDENTIFY the particular Executive Skills strengths of high performers at work, you can more easily see how yours come into play with theirs. With some practice, you can identify both strengths and weaknesses in office interactions as well as in dealings with customers or clients. More importantly, you can predict many interaction issues in advance, to your advantage either at the office or with customers.

If you're an executive or a manager, this knowledge could help you identify others who could become high performers in future situations, based on matching the strengths of the high performers currently in that or similar job functions to those of the person you're considering to move into that same job. For example, if you identify several high performers in a department and many of them have a specific Executive Skills strength, it's likely that the strength is useful or even required for success in that role. It's then likely that someone moving to that department who also is strong in the same skill will find success more easily than some-one who isn't, all other things being equal.

If you stop for a moment and visualize specific activities and behaviors you've witnessed in high performers around you at work, you can start to identify their Executive Skills. The method, of course, is to look for behaviors that likely associate with particular strengths and weaknesses.

The advantage of identifying Executive Skills in high performers is that you also could find similar strengths in those who may work in other areas but possess the same strengths as high performers in another department. This can provide a potential career path for you or someone who may not yet be in a high-performing situation.

To find these types of matches requires identifying the strengths needed for a certain role. Each department or organization may be different in terms of what strengths are needed for any given situation, but the results of our study may provide some help.

For example, high performers who work in customer service are strong in Organization or Flexibility. Those same skills are also most frequently found in high performers in administration, which could be an area where a person could be successful in either department.

It can work the other way as well. Since high performers in IT have different strengths (Planning/Prioritization) than those in customer service (Flexibility), it would be less likely that a high performer from IT would move to customer service and become a high performer there. It's possible, but not as likely. The same would be true for sales departments, since the strengths of high performers there (Working Memory) are different from those in customer service (Flexibility).

In either case, the key is to identify which Executive Skills are most frequently found in people in any given area of your business. Once you know this, it becomes easier to identify others with these same characteristics, thereby increasing the chance of success in the same or similar role by creating goodness-of-fit situations.

SCENARIO:
Christopher manages several employees in the finance department. Budgets are being planned for the next year and it's time to select the

lead on the project. The person chosen will lead a team to gather various financials from several departments around the company. It always gets hectic this time of year, especially with everybody stretched so thin. Last year, Christopher had Jaclyn take the lead, but things kept falling apart at the last minute. She was constantly overwhelmed and kept going back to Christopher asking him which reports he needed next, since she had so many and they all seemed critical to her. So this year, Christopher wants to select someone who can manage many things at the same time, especially since a lot of the numbers come in late. Christopher needs someone who can prioritize so the person doesn't have to keep coming back for advice on what's important. He recalls that every time Paige is at a meeting, she creates a checklist for to-do items following the meeting and that her list always seems logical, with the most important tasks listed first. So he selects Paige this year, and it ends up being dramatically smoother than last year, and Paige easily prioritizes the reports and keeps Christopher up-to-date on a regular basis.

While both Jaclyn and Paige are highly valued employees in Christopher's department, the specific task at hand—managing a complex budget process—requires the person have certain characteristics. Specifically, the person should be strong in the Executive Skill of Planning/Prioritization. In the case of Jaclyn last year, she no doubt is weak in that skill, which made it very difficult for her to prioritize when it got busy. For Paige, who is strong in Planning/Prioritization, it was very natural for her to determine which reports were more important than others at the time, as well as to create a methodical flow from all the departments. She also very naturally knew when to update Christopher, since at the start of the project she made a list of dates for the updates.

It's important to first identify Executive Skills that likely will be needed for a certain task or function before accepting that job or selecting a person for that function if you're a manager. If a certain set of tasks requires a lot of short, tight deadline deliverables, then a person strong in Task Initiation and Sustained Attention would be more likely to succeed than someone weak in those skills. A task or set of tasks that are long-term and goal-oriented, such as on a large, six-month-long project, would be best handled by someone strong in Goal-Directed Persistence. Placing a person who is strong in Task Initiation may get the job started on time but not hit the final target.

Unfortunately, sometimes a person is selected for various reasons that are hardly scientific. It might be that a person has been performing well in a certain role, so as a reward he or she is given a new, specific task. Unfortunately for both parties, the Executive Skills required for the new tasks are not the strengths that made the person successful in his or her previous role.

Shared Strengths in One Organization

Different departments and organizations have their own criteria to identify their high performers, as we described earlier. Matching those criteria to results from organizations often creates a correlation between the criteria used to define who's a high performer and the strengths of those individuals.

In our study, no executives or managers who selected the high performers were surprised by the results of the strengths and weaknesses of them, but viewing it in these terms gave them a new perspective to help them manage better. They often had different ways of describing their teams' characteristics and different terms for the strengths and weaknesses, though they were easily mapped to Executive Skills.

Alliance Member Services (AMS) Inc., a member-based organization that writes insurance coverage for nonprofits throughout the United States, serves nonprofits and brokers of all sizes by providing insurance at prices that they promote are adequate and fair, and that can be maintained over the long term.

These are the characteristics of high performers at AMS:

▪ Metacognition is a strength in the majority (60 percent) of high performers; no one is weak in it.

▪ Goal-Directed Persistence is a strength in half of the high performers; no one is weak in it.

- Working Memory is the third most common strength, found in almost a third of the high performers; no one is weak in it.

- For weaknesses, half are weak in Task Initiation, half are weak in Emotional Control, and 40 percent are weak in Response Inhibition.

Interestingly, the leading three strengths and weaknesses of high performers at AMS are the same as those in high performers in the financial services/real estate/insurance industries.

Pamela E. Davis, president and chief executive officer of AMS, and members of her team participated, and she agreed with the results, which she mapped to some of the characteristics at work that are associated with the particular Executive Skills found in her high performers.[1] Says Davis:

It makes sense to me that high performers in the insurance industry need to be strong in Metacognition because very little of what we do is tangible. Our "product" is a "promise to pay." My staff needs to be able to plan and execute on things that have no actual known value at the time we produce them. We work in a world of numbers, estimates, and probabilities, the validity of which only gets confirmed many years from the decision point. We have to be able to frame an anticipated outcome from a bunch of facts and ideas and evaluate progress, sometimes with very small bits of unreliable information.

For example, if we are working to develop a new product, we have to figure out what the risk of claims (both frequency and severity) for this new product will be when, in fact, we may have very little to go on to guide our pricing. We have to spend a lot of time thinking about the various different possible scenarios, none of which may ever come to pass. So a lot of what we do is just in our heads, although the actuaries will tell you that this is hard science.

I think that Goal-Directed Persistence comes into play here because we don't get the satisfaction of, say, seeing a car come off of the assembly line. In fact, because claims take years to develop, there may actually be little direct connection between our actions today and the financial performance for this year. So, we have to be very goal directed in terms of what we want to accomplish from a transaction basis.

As for Working Memory, insurance is a very detail-intense industry, with the various policy types and forms, most of them differing by company, with one company frequently offering multiple variations of the same policy forms. Practitioners in this field need to keep a lot of this in their heads.

As for Task Initiation, I have such a sense of urgency that I suppose my own leadership style has tended to compensate for whatever inclination might exist in my staff to procrastinate. I have no idea why a sense of urgency would not be important for those in finance/insurance, but maybe it goes again toward the long-range view before the results of actions are seen, so why rush? [The CEO is the only person who measured to be strong in Task Initiation.]

Regarding Emotional Control and Organization, insurance is considered to be a relationship business, and that part of this industry distracts us from getting our best work done. Maybe this even goes to the procrastination. Why spend a lot of time getting all the details to write a policy and compete on the merits if you can just go out on the golf course and seal the deal? I have witnessed a fair amount of politics at larger insurance organizations, but I don't tolerate that here. If Organization strengths can be considered to be the same as discipline, then in general, the insurance industry lacks discipline and operates cyclically, with prices varying widely in various cyclical periods. This is not because the cost of risk has changed but because the insurance companies convince themselves that they can make up inadequate premium prices in volume or through investment earnings, and over and over again, they get themselves into financial difficulty because they lack pricing discipline. This goes back to not really knowing—or at least being able to convince yourself—that you don't really know the ultimate cost of the policy you are selling.

Shared Strengths in Two Nonprofits

If you work in a nonprofit organization, there are other patterns you may notice. In two nonprofits in the study, high performers in both organizations have the same three most commonly found strengths and weaknesses, which were the same three most commonly found in nonprofits overall. The two nonprofits are in different categories and located in different parts of the United States. And if you don't work in a nonprofit but deal with some, this can show you what Executive Skills you can expect to encounter in the high performers who work there.

High performers at the United States Pony Clubs, Inc. (USPC), in Lexington, Kentucky, had some similarities with Alliance Member Services in their strengths and weaknesses.

- Planning/Prioritization is a strength in the majority (67 percent) of high performers.

- Goal-Directed Persistence is a strength in exactly half of high performers.

- Working Memory is a strength in half of high performers.

- Half of the high performers are weak in Sustained Attention, a third in Stress Tolerance, and a third in Task Initiation. None of these three skills is a strength in any of the high performers at USPC.

"I found the results to be very interesting and not too surprising based on the performance of my staff," says Peggy Entrekin, executive director of USPC.[2]

"My primary takeaway is identifying a frustration that I think a number of my staff members feel in not having much luck in initiation of tasks and ideas," says Entrekin. "I am somewhat surprised because that's not something I would have identified about all but one of my staff members. I suspect that this is fairly common among staff of nonprofit organizations where the staff implements programs determined by the board."

As was typical, the weaknesses found in high performers didn't seem to cause major problems, since the individuals possessing them are, in essence, successful. This was also found to be the case with USPC.

"Sustained Attention, which was found to be a weakness in half of our high performers, doesn't seem to be an issue for us because a task or project often has to sit on a staff member's desk while they wait for a volunteer to complete their part," says Entrekin.

"These study results will impact my hiring in the future," Entrekin says. "I can definitely see application to what I learned from it in ways to help support my staff going forward, and it has great application to any further assignment of duties and hiring opportunities."

Meanwhile, at the Shasta Women's Refuge in Redding, California, the three most commonly found Executive Skills strengths (Planning/ Prioritization, Goal-Directed Persistence, and Working Memory) are the same as the three most commonly found in high performers at USPC and in nonprofits overall. "I found the results generally not too surprising," says Executive Director Maggie John.[3] "Our leadership staff is very mission-driven (Goal-Directed Persistence), and the team has many complex tasks, including analytical grant tracking, understanding penal code applications, and directing staff on the proper tools for client assessment (Working Memory)."

The three weaknesses most commonly found at the organization were the same as those found in high performers in nonprofits overall. The three are Task Initiation, Stress Tolerance, and Sustained Attention.

"For some reason we are always up against a deadline," says John. "For example, while I'm typing this, I'm waiting for some information from staff for a grant that is due tomorrow. As to Stress Tolerance, the nature of the work is very stressful. The team has to concern themselves with not only their own stress but also that of their staff. Compassion fatigue is an occupational hazard."

Mapping Characteristics to Executive Skills

In addition to sharing the high performers' results of participating organizations with them, we analyzed the characteristics of how organizations selected their high performers against the study results of their high performers. Since many of the characteristics identified can be matched to certain Executive Skills, this may be helpful for you to see how to map your own high-performing criteria to specific Executive Skills.

For example, you may be like those in one organization that identifies its high performers as problem solvers who keep their eye on strategic goals. The Executive Skill most closely related to keeping an eye on strategic goals is Goal-Directed Persistence. And it turns out that the majority of high performers from that organization were found to be strong in Goal-Directed Persistence. This would make them more likely to keep their eye on the long-term or strategic goals, which is precisely how the organization defined its high performers.

Likewise, in another organization that identifies its high performers as those who are forward-looking and results-oriented, those high performers also were found to be strong in Goal-Directed Persistence.

From a practical standpoint, a department or an organization should not attempt to fill slots with all people strong in the same Executive Skill, since that could cause some imbalance. Most notably, a set of other Executive Skills strengths would likely be missing. If every person in a department was strong in Goal-Directed Persistence, for example, long-term objectives and goals may be top of mind, while day-to-day and shorter-term projects fall by the wayside, since many likely would be weak in Task Initiation, a commonly found opposite in those strong in Goal-Directed Persistence.

One company selects its high performers based on successfully managing multiple tasks, so the key Executive Skill needed would not be Goal-Directed Persistence but rather Organization to be able to keep track of those tasks. In that company, the majority of high performers who participated in our study were strong in Organization.

Another business identifies its high performers as those who are accurate and handle stress well. All the high performers from that organization were strong in either Working Memory or Planning/Prioritization, and none were weak in Stress Tolerance. Strong Working Memory would make it more likely for high performers there to be accurate by easily recalling important details during a hectic day.

Another organization defines its high performers as those who are creative in moving the organization forward. The majority of high performers there were strong in either Flexibility or Metacognition, Executive Skills often associated with creativity.

The point is you can relatively easily map the criteria for selecting high performers to the actual Executive Skills strengths of those high performers. This means you should be able to map the skills of high performers around you to certain Executive Skills strengths and see which positions are the best fit for your own strengths.

Avoiding Potential Conflicts

One of the great benefits in identifying Executive Skills strengths and weaknesses in others is to get the right person doing the right task and avoid mismatches of people to activities. Without this knowledge, it's very easy for a person to end up in what is inherently the wrong task. When there's a mismatch of Executive Skills of a person to the task, it may be doable, but it will be inherently difficult. In many cases, the task will not be done to the satisfaction of the person assigning it and will not feel rewarding for the person doing it.

It's also true that when two people have different Executive Skills strengths and weaknesses, they tend to look at things differently. If you're strong in Time Management, you may view a person low in that skill to be rude coming to a meeting late, while the person weak in Time Management sees it as no big deal, since he was only ten minutes late. Time is viewed differently by the two people.

SCENARIO: LATE STARTING

Kyle is one of the most productive people in the marketing department. Not only is his work top-notch, but it seems to always get better. When he directs research programs, he always advances the results from the previous research, frequently remembering that little detail that could make or break the research results. He also always knows what to tackle next, even if he doesn't tackle it right away. But it really bugs Michaela, the vice president of the company, that when she wants a quick update on the latest campaign, she always has to wait because it never seems to yet be under way. And with all the work to do these days, it infuriates Michaela when she sees Kyle sitting at his desk seemingly just staring into space or at the ceiling. Michaela finally confronts Kyle and tells him he needs to get started on research and campaigns as soon as they are assigned. She also chides him for what she calls daydreaming during work and tells Kyle he needs to stay focused on his work.

While Kyle's Executive Skills strengths are a match for the job, they're different from the strengths of Michaela, and therein lies the problem. Kyle is strong in Metacognition, so the creative part of the marketing campaigns continually improves. While he may appear to be daydreaming, Kyle is actually reflecting on ways to improve on the marketing messages for his clients. Michaela mistakes Kyle's thinking and development process to daydreaming, based on appearance to her. She also is more focused on short-term results, being strong in Task Initiation, so she equates starting right away with doing the job effectively, because that's how she'd tend to do it. Michaela should more closely analyze the effectiveness and success of Kyle's work rather than her perceptions of what he does moment to moment, unless, of course, it becomes a departmental distraction. However, this would be unlikely, since Kyle's strength in Metacognition would make it quite natural for him to continually find ways to improve on his marketing goals, as well as the work of those he works with.

As in the previous scenario, a typical combination of Executive Skills of high performers in marketing departments is strong Metacognition and weak Task Initiation.

Focus on Executive Skills Strengths

While Executive Skills strengths and weaknesses can be identified in individuals, it's what happens after that becomes critical.

When hiring someone, it's natural to select a person based on his or her perceived strengths. Then the next period of time, perhaps even a period of years, is spent trying to correct that person's weaknesses. It's easy to gloss over issues that are going smoothly and focus on those that need work. It's only natural.

The good news is that in performance reviews, the majority of business leaders say their organizations spend more time focusing on strengths rather than on weaknesses (see Survey Results: Strengths and Weaknesses). However, those same executives and managers are not totally successful at correcting those problems, with only 4 percent saying they've been extremely successful, although a majority say they're somewhat successful.

SURVEY RESULTS: STRENGTHS AND WEAKNESSES

When it comes to discussing a person's strengths over weaknesses in a typical performance review, how much time does your department and/or organization spend focusing on strengths over weaknesses?

Significantly more on strengths	14%
Somewhat more on strengths	40%
Same on strengths and weaknesses	26%
Somewhat less on strengths	15%
Significantly less on strengths	4%

After a typical performance review, how successful do you think executives and/or managers are in getting subordinates to correct their weaknesses?

Extremely successful	4%
Somewhat successful	67%
Somewhat unsuccessful	24%
Extremely unsuccessful	5%

Voices from the Front Lines: Strengths and Weaknesses

"Not everyone believes in positive reinforcement, and it is always a lot easier to point out what's going bad than giving a pat on the back and saying what's good about an employee (it almost seems as though the strengths are a given and there is no need to reiterate them, while weaknesses need to be specified thoroughly if management wants them to be improved)."

"Most people are aware of their strengths because they have experienced success and get some feedback. It is important that people are able to personally identify their weaknesses, because a weakness cannot be addressed without acknowledgment."

"The validity of managing strengths and weaknesses depends on how objectively you measure performance outcomes. You may discover that some people are simply in the wrong positions—their executive skills do not mesh with the job performance requirements. An individual's ability to improve also depends on whether the training, coaching, mentoring, and opportunities available to them actually help improve their job execution."

"People only want to hear how great they are."

"How much time you spend on strengths and weaknesses is completely dependent on how strong the person is and how serious they are about working on their areas for improvement. Most people either don't want to or are not able to significantly improve on their weaknesses. In my career, I can count on one hand how many individuals have truly made significant strides in eliminating their weaknesses."

"The key to getting the most out of staff is to focus on their strengths. Working on weaknesses is a joint effort of the manager and the employee. The manager must have a clear understanding of the employee and help them create solutions for weaknesses—which may mean finding work-arounds that pull in their strengths to overcome their weaker areas."

Healthcare: Clinical vs. Nonclinical

Earlier, we detailed strengths and weaknesses by department. Among the broad range of categories, we singled out healthcare, which we wanted to be able to segment into two parts, clinical and nonclinical. We figure that someone who provides medical care may have different cognitive characteristics from those who work in the business or administration end of a hospital, and we did find differences in Executive Skills in high performers based on whether they worked in clinical or nonclinical departments.

In clinical departments, the most commonly found Executive Skills strength is Organization, and the most common strength in nonclinical areas of healthcare is Working Memory. While two of the three skills (Organization and Planning/Prioritization) are among the three most commonly found skills in both groups, the number-one skill found is different for each. There also is one notable difference.

- *Strengths—Clinical:* Organization, Planning/Prioritization, Task Initiation

- *Strengths—Nonclinical:* Working Memory, Planning/Prioritization, Organization

In clinical departments, Task Initiation is one of the three most commonly found strengths of high performers. In nonclinical departments, not only is it among one of the fewest found strengths, but it is also the leading weakness in high performers.

This information could be useful if you work in a clinical department and have ambitions to move into the business side of a hospital or other area of healthcare at some point. If you're strong in Task Initiation, it won't be harmful in a nonclinical role, but it's not a necessary Executive Skill to be a high performer there. However, it's likely that if you're a clinical high performer you're also strong in either Organization or Planning/Prioritization, both among the three most commonly found skills in nonclinical areas, which could be of help.

But the great advantage would go to the person in a clinical department who's strong in Working Memory, of which there are a number, though not as many as possess the other strengths noted, since that's the most commonly found strength of high performers in nonclinical healthcare departments.

And a healthcare executive planning to transfer someone from a clinical area to the business side, which does occur, could also use this knowledge. Since Task Initiation is not a critical strength for those in nonclinical areas of healthcare, at least in high-performing individuals, the executive could seek out the person with strong Working Memory.

- *Weaknesses—Clinical:* Stress Tolerance, Emotional Control, Goal-Directed Persistence

- *Weaknesses—Nonclinical:* Task Initiation, Stress Tolerance, Emotional Control

Whether they're in clinical or nonclinical areas of healthcare, high performers have two weaknesses in common, Emotional Control and Stress Tolerance. This could make a person feel defensive about a negative comment someone makes in the course of a day, and this could bother her for hours if not days. She also could become emotionally stressed in a crisis situation and is more comfortable with a routine.

Both of these weaknesses are common opposites to Organization, a common strength in both clinical and nonclinical areas.

High Performers in Sales-Buyer Interactions

In addition to identifying Executive Skills in people you work with, you also can identify them in your clients and customers, with an eye toward improving interactions with them. Sales is one clear example, where the first step is to know the strengths of the salesperson.

Once a high-performing salesperson or sales manager understands his or her inherent strengths or weaknesses, it's easier to determine potential interactions with customers or clients with other, different strengths and weaknesses.

For example, if salespeople strong in Flexibility can quickly identify a potential customer with the same strength, they're more likely to have a positive interaction as the salespeople lead the customer through a myriad of potential sales options. A weak Flexibility buyer is much less likely to be open to considering many choices. However, since many high-performing salespeople are strong in Flexibility, it would be effortless for them to adapt to the inflexible buyer.

Fortunately, there are ways for salespeople to identify at least several Executive Skills strengths or weaknesses in people as they go through the buying process.

Over the course of a year, we conducted two major field studies to determine if certain Executive Skills could be observed during the purchasing process. The first study[4] was to determine whether specific Executive Skills associated with impulse behavior could be accurately observed in consumers during the purchasing process, and the second[5] was to determine whether certain Executive Skills could be observed during the process of buying televisions and other high-end electronics.

Impulse buyers are scattered about any market, where they look to fulfill a basic need for instant gratification. Marketers continually try to pinpoint who these consumers are, what they look like, and how to get them to almost effortlessly decide to buy their product. Many retailers can figure out which items are the impulse items, even if just by trial and error, and place those items near the checkout. The Holy Grail, however, is to identify who it is who's likely to buy those products every time. Potential impulse buyers can be identified based on Executive Skills that can be observed within a very short period of time, sometimes in fewer than 60 seconds. This can be of enormous value to you if you are in sales.

Response Inhibition and Flexibility are the skills most observable during the purchasing process.[6] The study's teams observed buyers in the purchasing process and determined if the consumers appeared to be strong or weak in the skill.[7]

Once you know the behaviors, it becomes relatively easy to determine if the shopper is strong or weak in either of the two Executive Skills.[8] The researchers could, with a high degree of certainty, match behaviors or actions with a specific Executive Skill.

If you're a high-performing salesperson, you're likely strong in Working Memory or Flexibility. If Working Memory is your strength, you'd be likely to identify specific behaviors of the shopper and match them to impulse or nonimpulse behaviors based on past interactions with other buyers. And if Flexibility is your strength, you'd easily adapt to accommodate the impulse or nonimpulse buyer.

This can be useful if you sell big-ticket items or services, since the higher the price, the easier it is to identify behaviors that relate to the two Executive Skills.[9] The teams researched at Target, Sears, Best Buy, Wal-Mart, Circuit City, and Tweeter[10] and validated their observations.[11]

Observable Behaviors

Here's a guide for high performers (or any salespeople, for that matter), with descriptions to identify specific behaviors in retail, grouped by Executive Skill. One or more of these behaviors in a person shopping are likely to be good indicators of the specific high or low Executive Skill noted.[12]

STRONG FLEXIBILITY: TYPICAL BEHAVIORS

A shopper high in Flexibility exhibits this both by actions that can be seen and by interactions with salespeople:

- Browses around looking at different items

- Walks around the store going from one side to the other and then back again for different items

- Makes a quick change to a similar item when an item is out of stock

- Doesn't stop to look at specific brands of food but just picks any brand

- Is open to suggestions from sales associates

- Tends to choose another product when the original is unavailable

- Tries to decide between a few similar items and then makes a decision

- Debates on two items and chooses the store brand because it's on sale

- Buys the brand recommended by the sales associate

- Is easily swayed by other suggestions

These potential buyers are likely to be quite open to your suggestions if you are a salesperson. They tend to seek you out to help guide them through a purchase decision and even ask for your suggestions as to what their preferences are, as well as ask what they should buy.[13] These buyers also tend to be highly interactive. They'll seek you out and ask many questions and take the time to describe the type of product they're looking for. They have little brand loyalty.[14]

If you're a high-performing salesperson strong in Flexibility, you can easily interact with the high Flexibility buyer. The challenge, though, is that since both of you are so adaptable, closing the sale or the deal should be your goal, more likely a trait to be found in high-performing sales managers or sales executives, based on our study. If you're a salesperson weak in Flexibility, you also can do well with a high Flexibility buyer since the buyer can easily come around to your suggestions.

WEAK FLEXIBILITY: TYPICAL BEHAVIORS
Shoppers weak in Flexibility appear to be somewhat determined in their buying behavior. This is signaled when consumers refuse to alter their

predetermined item. If the specific model they want is unavailable, they won't accept substitutions and they don't easily divert from plans. You may see a person walk into a store with a piece of paper with specifications written down. After discovering that this item isn't available, the shopper will refuse to switch to another substitutable product. Or the shopper may refuse your help; the shopper may abruptly interrupt you to say he isn't interested and continue further with his shopping. You are not likely to change this person's mind; realizing this can save you some wasted time.

A shopper weak in Flexibility can exhibit one or more of the following actions:

- Doesn't buy a product after examining it

- Appears to be on a mission

- Does not get distracted by gimmicks or displays

- Asks an employee for an exact product

- Walks directly to a particular item/department with little attention paid to other items/departments on the way

- Tends to leave the store when the desired product is not available

- Won't be persuaded when salesmen make recommendations or will deny a salesperson's help altogether

- Is stubborn and difficult to persuade

- Is focused and won't buy a substitute product if the intended product is not available

Brand loyalty is a common characteristic of weak Flexibility buyers, who tend to be determined about a product and even energetic about it. They'll consider only the item they came for, and if the store is out of what they want, they leave. They tend to look for one specific brand and leave if that branded product is not available. In interactions with you, they'll tend not to listen to your suggestions and ignore your recommendations, no matter how they sound. They're only interested in a particular product, and are not open to looking at different brands or models.

These potential buyers are noninteractive and generally don't want to speak to you or anyone else who works at the store. They usually won't approach you and typically respond to you saying they're just browsing or just looking. They're often apprehensive about different brands and have a list of preferred features. They tend to look at a small number of items and may appear to listen to you but don't take your advice.

If you're a high-performing salesperson strong in Flexibility, Working Memory, or Metacognition, you can easily identify this type of buyer because you probably remember seeing such buyers in the past, though you may not have known they could be identified by specific Executive Skills. You're more likely to have devised ways to interact with these buyers through trial and error (high Metacognition) and adapted your own behavior (Flexibility) to better accommodate these buyers. If you're weak in Flexibility, interacting with a weak Flexibility buyer should be brief, since the buyer is fixed on what he or she wants to buy and you are fixed on what you want to sell.

STRONG RESPONSE INHIBITION: TYPICAL BEHAVIORS

Consumers strong in Response Inhibition exhibit a distinct body language and know exactly what they're initially entering a store for. They walk in a fast-paced motion. They may listen to your advice and consider it but will most likely not change their mind unless you can convince them or provide enough facts to overturn their viewpoint. They don't respond well to sales or gimmicks and aren't usually worth pursuing for long periods of time.

During the buying process, a person strong in Response Inhibition will likely exhibit one or several of the following:

- Notices a discount bin but doesn't make a purchase

- Demonstrates hesitation toward making a purchase

- Picks up and puts back a product

- Does not browse other products

- Sees products on sale but doesn't buy

- Sticks with original purchase item when offered something on sale

- Picks up items and adds to cart but then puts them back

- Compares brands and, after contemplation, decides not to purchase

You are not likely to influence strong Response Inhibition shoppers. They'll listen but will be reserved about the actual idea of purchasing. They won't give in to you or take your advice. If they do interact, they may ask you a lot of questions to get the deal that best suits them, since they've done research before shopping and don't buy until they compare prices and consult with others.[15]

If you're a salesperson strong in Response Inhibition, you have an advantage with the high Response Inhibition buyer in the Executive Skills strengths of Flexibility and Metacognition.

If you're a salesperson strong in Flexibility, you'd be able to objectively analyze what it is the customer wants and be adaptable enough to provide either that product or service and close the deal. If you're strong in Working Memory, you readily recall similar situations with other self-restraint buyers and instantly remember the success rate and may decide not to invest much time with the buyer based on those recollections.

WEAK RESPONSE INHIBITION: TYPICAL BEHAVIORS

Shoppers weak in Response Inhibition are likely to act on impulse, with one indicator being abrupt stopping when they see a product that catches their eye, thus changing their pace and motivation.

The low Response Inhibition consumer will tend to show one or more of the following actions:

- Takes random products while walking around

- Appears to be distracted or scattered, picking up items without pattern

- Picks up something, puts it back, then goes back to it again and purchases it

- Tends to purchase complementary products around what he or she is buying

- Purchases an item that wasn't originally planned

- Walks down an aisle, notices a sale item, grabs it right away, puts it down, gives it a second glance, then takes a step back to pick it back up again

- Cannot walk by a sales table without buying an item

- Sees display for the item, then purchases it

- Buys more than planned

Weak Response Inhibition buyers are driven by what looks like impulse and tends to make purchases and decisions quickly.[16]

You can easily persuade them and easily sell a product they didn't necessarily want or need when they came into the store. The catch is if buyers are weak in the Executive Skill of Emotional Control, they are likely to have second thoughts after a purchase and may become so upset that they return the product later.

This is just one example of how if you are a high performer you may interact with buyers. It's natural that high performers have either instinctively or through a series of trial-and-error engagements determined the most effective ways to use their Executive Skills strengths to succeed, since they have.

▪ ▪ ▪

You've now seen how Executive Skills come into play at work, when interacting with others inside the organization as well as clients and customers outside. Being able to identify strengths and weaknesses of others based on their behaviors can help you figure the best ways to interact with them. You can see where your strengths compensate for their weaknesses and when their strengths compensate for yours. You can use this information to avoid conflicts, knowing that opposite strengths can cause two people to process or look at information or activity in totally different ways.

This knowledge also can help you identify which Executive Skills are needed in jobs based on the level, whether employee, manager, or executive, which we explore in the next chapter.

Avoiding the Wrong Promotion

Sorting the Strengths of Employees vs. Managers vs. Executives

WHILE KNOWING your Executive Skills strengths and weaknesses in advance can help you determine if your potential next move is the correct one, taking first-time right-seating to the next step involves making the correct move every time throughout your career.

The catch is that if you're a high performer who's in the right seat now, you'd tend to be successful over time, and that success often will be noticed by those above. When another opportunity comes along, another challenge with greater responsibilities, it's natural to tap the successful person and promote or move him or her into this new position without again checking whether it's another right-seating situation. It's instinctive and commonly accepted to reward success with a promotion when it becomes available.

Problems often occur because the person is not a fit for that next position, whether deserving of it or not, and through no fault of his or her own.

And when the promotion or transfer of a successful, high-performing individual becomes a dismal failure, nobody wins. The successful position has been vacated by the high performer and the new position is vacant again, and the process has to start over, potentially for both positions. You may have faced such a situation or probably know of at least one case of someone this happened to, where a person was doing well in one position, was moved, and then didn't do well in the new position. While the person's strengths were a perfect match for the old job, the new job required totally different Executive Skills.

Almost all business leaders today know of a case where a high-performing individual became a low performer in a different position (see Survey Results: High and Low Performers). In large companies, those with 10,000 or more employees, 97 percent of business leaders know of such a situation.

This indicates there's a common perception that a high performer can be promoted into what becomes less than a mirror of the previous success. We believe these situations can be minimized or avoided by identifying and matching Executive Skills strengths of the person to the new position.

The converse can also be true: That is, if you're a low performer, perhaps because of an Executive Skills mismatch in your current position, you can move into a position that plays to your strengths and become a high performer. Of course, it isn't natural to promote a person not doing well in his or her current job, though sometimes a transfer occurs and the person coincidentally ends up in a goodness-of-fit situation. By using first-time right-seating in every move, those coincidental successes can be replaced by those that are more predictive.

The opinions on whether an "average" business individual can become a high performer are almost evenly split, with only slightly more than half of executives and managers thinking they can (see Survey Results: High and Low Performers). More managers than top executives say they think an "average" business individual can become a high performer.

It could depend where you get moved to that determines whether you become or continue to be a high performer. In various departments, there are differences in the most commonly found Executive Skills in employees, managers, and executives within each of those specific departments, several of which we detail later in this chapter, which could help explain both situations.

SURVEY RESULTS: HIGH AND LOW PERFORMERS

In your experience, how likely is it that an "average" individual in business can develop into a high performer?

Extremely likely	7%
Somewhat likely	48%
Somewhat unlikely	35%
Extremely unlikely	10%

Do you know of anyone who was a high performer in one position who became a low performer in another?

Yes	82%
No	18%

Voices from the Front Lines: High and Low Performers

"It is very sad when inexperienced managers promote a top performer into a role for which they are unsuited and that individual becomes a failure."

"I have seen people placed in the wrong job for their talents and when they move to the job that lets them use their talents, they can be a high performer in that particular role."

"The truly exceptional high performers are rare. If these individuals are in the right situation, they can perform far beyond their peers. However, in the wrong situations, they will be resented by their average or subpar peers, rather than admired."

"Having a high-performance employee starts at the hiring process. In 30 years of supervising managers and directors, when I have to deal with a problem employee, I can almost always trace the problem to the hiring process."

"It's all about fit—and high performers have an innate ability to pick roles where they can leverage their strengths and excel."

"Being a high performer is something that is innate. It can be refined, nurtured, and developed, but not instilled. If you have employees that don't have it, don't expect it."

"The change from average to high performer is possible but not usual."

The Failed Sales Promotion

Promotions often are a reward for past success. The best manager becomes a director, or the most successful director at a field office becomes a vice president. But in sales departments, the promotion pattern is sometimes highly pronounced and visible to many because salespeople often are well known in many organizations.

Businesses typically can identify a strong salesperson based on past performance in any given marketplace. Salespeople in one industry generally know who in sales in that market is good, since many are competing for the same sale, and it ultimately becomes obvious who won by who closed the deal or made the sale. In many cases at the retail level, success can be tracked by the size of the sales commissions handed out to salespeople.

In either case, it can be relatively easy to gauge success over time. Sometimes it's because of a superior product or service, but sometimes it's due to how that product or service was sold. More precisely, it's *who* sold it and how the salesperson interacted with the buyer. Whether in a business-to-business or business-to-consumer transaction, the Executive Skills of the person doing the selling, as well as of those doing the buying, can play a role.

While there are certain strengths common across high performers in sales at all levels, from employee to executive, there are some differences. This is important because great salespeople often are promoted into sales management, where some succeed and some don't.

However, there's a way to more accurately predict which salesperson is likely to be successful in management. This is one more way to help determine which salesperson has the greatest chance to succeed in sales management. If you're in sales, it also could provide a tool for career planning.

As a group comprising employees, managers, and executives, high performers in sales are strong in Working Memory, Goal-Directed Persistence, Planning/Prioritization, and Flexibility. This means they typically can do one task without losing sight of other commitments, are reliable, can be counted on to follow through, and are able to keep their eye on the ball. They're able to achieve long-term goals, are task-focused, and can be relied on for task completion. They're independent, have a high tolerance for ambiguity, can integrate new information, and are adaptable to changing course, which is frequently required in sales situations.

For people in sales departments, by age, the top strength is Working Memory both for people from 20 to 30 years old and for those from 51 to 60.

The weakest skills of high performers in sales as a group are Task Initiation, Organization, and Emotional Control. This would indicate that they tend to procrastinate and can be slow to get started, tend to be messy and lose things, or can be emotional and sensitive to criticism, whether they show it or not.

So these are characteristics common to all high-performing salespeople, including sales employees, managers, and executives. But the real potential lies in identifying similarities and differences in characteristics among employees, managers, and executives.

Not only is it common for successful salespeople to be promoted into sales management, but it's also generally perceived to be a logical course of action. In fact, a majority of senior executives and managers think a successful salesperson can become a successful sales manager or sales executive (see Survey Results: Promoting Salespeople into Management).

The great irony is that while most business leaders believe great salespeople can succeed in management, most of them can identify a case where the promoted salesperson didn't work out. There's something almost instinctive that executives and managers know about making these promotions, in expecting that they won't all work out.

However, this sixth sense doesn't generally stop a promotion from occurring. "My experience is that good salespersons do not typically make good managers," says one executive who responded to the survey. "It is a very different skill set." Says another: "In my career I have found few instances where a great salesperson became a great sales manager. It seems when you put the title *manager* to a very productive salesperson, they change in such a way that makes them ineffective as a leader."

It's not likely that the *salesperson* changed once becoming a sales manager; it's more that *the requirements for the job* changed. It could be that the requirements of the management position are different from the requirements of the sales employee position, not demanding the same strengths that could have contributed to the success of the sales employee. And when an organization promotes its top salesperson into sales management and the person doesn't succeed, the company has lost not only a manager, but one of its best salespeople as well, making it even more critical that the person with the best chance of success be identified.

SURVEY RESULTS: PROMOTING SALESPEOPLE INTO MANAGEMENT

In general, how likely do you think a successful salesperson would become a successful sales manager or sales executive?

Extremely likely	8%
Somewhat likely	67%
Somewhat unlikely	23%
Extremely unlikely	2%

In your career, do you know of any case where a sales employee was promoted into sales management and did not succeed in the new role?

Yes	86%
No	14%

Voices from the Front Lines: Promoting Salespeople to Management

"Effective selling and effective management require different skills. But the ability to convince others to buy something is generally a very positive attribute in a manager as well."

"It does not automatically follow that a successful sales or tech person will be a successful manager. It seems a recurring lesson that every industry and discipline needs to learn and relearn."

"Some successful salespeople are great leaders, but the skill sets have minimal overlap."

"Excellent salespeople most often do not make excellent managers; their outlooks and priorities are just much different."

"It depends on the personality of the individual and whether or not they are capable of a management role to begin with."

"Managing sales and actual selling takes a different skill set. It is possible for someone to have both, but in my experience [it is] not likely."

"Many times people are promoted into management positions based on success in different areas and many times this is disastrous, as there is a very specific skill set to manage successfully."

"Management skills are quite different when compared to sales skills. One does not equate with the other by extension. Why lose a good salesperson and risk getting a poor manager?"

"I have seen someone excel in sales. However, they were not able to manage people once they were promoted to sales manager."

"The characteristics that make an excellent salesperson do not often reside in the same body as the required skills of a competent sales manager. Unfortunately, this fact is not widely known. I've seen too many situations where companies lost their best salesperson and subsequent second- and third-best salespeople by promoting from within."

"An excellent salesperson may not have the skills to be an excellent sales manager."

Sales Employees vs. Sales Management

There are differences between the strengths of high-performing sales employees and sales managers, which could help explain why a great salesperson is promoted and fails.

For employees, the most frequently found strengths are Working Memory, Metacognition, and Flexibility. The fourth strength is Planning/Prioritization in about a third of employees, more than four times the number of sales employees who have this as one of their weakest skills. A very small percentage of high-performing sales employees are strong in Sustained Attention, Time Management, Task Initiation, or Emotional Control. In fact, the leading weaknesses in high-performing salespeople are Task Initiation, Organization, and Emotional Control, making them likely to get upset when they do not make a sale.

This combination of strengths would seem logical, as sales employees find themselves having to adapt in many situations while interacting with clients or customers. Being strong in Flexibility allows them to more naturally go with the flow in any given situation and adapt to a customer's needs. Being strong in Working Memory allows them to easily recall past interactions and previous sales experiences, product and service information, and even what they promised a customer in an earlier encounter. Being strong in Metacognition allows salespeople to very naturally reflect on a just-completed sale to review how they personally performed and how they could do even better next time around.

Executive Skills Strengths: Sales Employees

Working Memory

Metacognition

Flexibility

Executive Skills Weaknesses: Sales Employees

Task Initiation

Emotional Control

Organization

The most commonly found strength across all three levels of sales—employee, manager, and executive—is Working Memory. This skill would make it likely that issues do not become forgotten in the heat of a sale, no matter the level of salesperson. Interestingly, of all high performers strong in Working Memory, more are in sales than in any other department.

But a key difference between the levels of sales is that high-performing sales managers and executives are more goal-oriented and focused. This is because Goal-Directed Persistence is the second most commonly found skill in both managers and executives and not among the most frequently found in employees in sales, being only the sixth out of 12 most frequently found skills. More than two times more high-performing executives than sales employees are strong in Goal-Directed Persistence, and almost no high-performing sales executives are weak in the skill.

So while it appears that sales employees are always on the lookout to improve how they sell (strong Metacognition) and easily can adapt to client changes (strong Flexibility), many of them will not naturally be good at defining and achieving goals, a role much better suited to high-performing managers and executives in sales.

This means if you're a sales employee and one of your strengths is Goal-Directed Persistence, you have a higher probability of being a high-performing sales manager or executive than others. A certain percentage of high-performing sales employees are strong in Goal-Directed Persistence, but it's far from one of the most commonly found strengths.

High performers in sales share many more weaknesses across titles than they do strengths. Many employees, managers, and executives all are weak in Task Initiation and Organization, both skills being among the most frequently found weaknesses in all three groups. And the higher a person is by sales level, the less likely that projects will be naturally started by them, since three out of five high-performing sales executives count Task Initiation as a weakness, much more than people at the other two levels.

MOST FREQUENTLY FOUND EXECUTIVE SKILLS STRENGTHS: SALES

Employees	Managers	Executives
Working Memory	Working Memory	Working Memory
Metacognition	Goal-Directed Persistence	Goal-Directed Persistence
Flexibility	Planning/Prioritization	Flexibility

MOST FREQUENTLY FOUND EXECUTIVE SKILLS WEAKNESSES: SALES

Employees	Managers	Executives
Task Initiation	Task Initiation	Task Initiation
Emotional Control	Emotional Control	Organization
Organization	Organization	Time Management

This could be one reason that a successful salesperson, one who can easily adapt (Flexibility), naturally track customers and customer interactions (Working Memory), or keep improving to increase sales (Metacognition), doesn't always do so well after a promotion to management.

In the new role, that same person may be required to track multiple salespeople and their performance and successes, make sure that a sales team meets certain targets, and plan for the next quarter and annual targets (Goal-Directed Persistence). That manager or executive may have to be more goal-oriented and stay focused on the aggregate sales numbers rather than a particular sale with one client or customer. This is less natural for someone not strong in Goal-Directed Persistence and even more difficult for someone weak in it, which could make the difference between success and failure in a sales promotion.

The good news is that there are a number of high-performing sales employees strong in Goal-Directed Persistence, though it's not commonly found. So the strategy or approach for consideration of moving an employee-level salesperson to sales management is to identify those strong in Goal-Directed Persistence in advance. This can be done during the hiring process, so that you know well in advance the sales management potential before the person even starts at the sales employee level.

This same approach can be used with other departments as well, once you know which Executive Skills strengths are most commonly found at the management level compared to the employee level, which we identify later in this chapter. You can match your skills by level to see where you might best fit.

And if you're a manager, promoting sales employees strong in Goal-Directed Persistence into sales management doesn't absolutely guarantee success, but it does substantially increase the chances of success. When you do this, it creates a goodness-of-fit situation, so that the strengths the people were born with match the job functions that they'll be required to perform.

Because a smaller percentage of high-performing sales employees are strong in Goal-Directed Persistence, there are likely to be fewer of them at any given department or organization. That being the case, once you've identified a sales employee strong in that skill, it would be in the interest of the organization to cultivate and compensate that individual as an investment in the future.

Working in a Comfort Zone

Even if high performance could be accurately predicted in advance, the question is, What would you or an organization do about it, considering inertia and comfort? For example, you may become comfortable with what you're doing, especially after you learn well what you do and achieve success doing it. You can fall into a comfort zone from which you don't want to leave.

In addition, the majority of senior executives and managers say they're satisfied in their current position (see Survey Results: Job Satisfaction). When it comes to job satisfaction, 82 percent of executives and managers are satisfied, and relatively few are dissatisfied. So there's the issue of risking current satisfaction for an unknown.

It also could be that you already have the strengths that best match the skills needed in your position so you find yourself feeling comfortable doing what you do. This is another reason a salesperson could be very successful and then get talked into accepting a promotion into sales management and fail.

Of course, part of the reason people can be satisfied at work is because of the people they work with. "When you're surrounded by hardworking and caring people, work is a joy," says one manager and survey respondent. At times, even when business or markets are challenging, the people others work with can keep them going. "Working in an industry that's in the midst of dynamic change is exciting, but it is the quality of people with whom I work that helps sustain my satisfaction level," says another manager.

Perhaps a more accurate reflection of people working well together involves the similarities and complementing nature of their Executive Skills strengths and weaknesses because that is what could determine their interactions with each other. If the high performers in one group in a particular department all are weak in, say, Task Initiation but strong in Goal-Directed Persistence, they collectively might not be bothered by a task or project not being started immediately, since they all realize that they and their coworkers will get it done when it needs to be done because they all ultimately deliver. Conversely, a manager strong in Task Initiation and weak in Goal-Directed Persistence is likely to get annoyed at someone who doesn't start the task or project immediately, since that would be a more natural process for that manager, who would expect others to behave the same way.

SURVEY RESULTS: JOB SATISFACTION

When it comes to my level of satisfaction in my current position today, I am:

Extremely satisfied	35%
Somewhat satisfied	47%
Somewhat dissatisfied	13%
Extremely dissatisfied	5%

Voices from the Front Lines: Job Satisfaction

"My personal satisfaction in my work is related to the fact that I provide a service that has value and I choose who I want to work with. If I encounter a prospective client that doesn't get the value, I nicely explain that I am not the best person to engage with and refer them to organizations that offer a similar service but on a commodity basis."

"I work in IT (where working WAS a pleasure) with some of the brightest people in the industry. Too bad we all are terribly underutilized, and many of the talent simply gets lost (and bored) right out the door. It's really sad."

"I have the privilege of working for a company whose goal is to be one of the Top 20 Best Companies to Work for in America. We're still trying to make it to the Top 100 on the *Forbes* list, but the good news is, our CEO takes employee morale and everyone's job satisfaction very seriously. That kind of attitude at the top is remarkably gratifying for the rest of us in management."

"We move people without taking into consideration the impact this has on family, and life outside of work. Also I hear about work/life balance, but does anyone really care about that these days or is it all talk?"

"I enjoy my job and working with my staff. However, currently, I feel as if I receive no upper management support and it makes my job somewhat difficult and at times unbearable."

IT Executives Can Shield the Heat

Both high-performing employees and executives who work in information technology departments are likely to continually review their processes and technology deployments, since Metacognition is the most commonly found strength in both groups. This strength also would make it less likely for high performers in IT to repeat the same mistake, since those strong in Metacognition tend to naturally review just-completed work to evaluate how to do it better next time. For high-performing executives in IT, not only is Metacognition the most frequently found strength, but 95 percent of executives do not count it as a weakness.

Meanwhile, high-performing IT managers would easily identify what's important and what's not and be natural at sequencing logical events in the proper order, since the most commonly found strength in IT managers is Planning/Prioritization. Many of them also may seem somewhat reserved and thoughtful, as they tend to think before they speak rather than just shoot from the hip. This is because the second most commonly found skill in managers is Response Inhibition. They also would tend to be adaptable to changes, since many of them are strong in Flexibility, just slightly more than the number of those strong in Metacognition.

In Executive Skills weaknesses, there's a notable difference between employees and managers compared to executives. The most commonly found weakness in both employees and managers is Stress Tolerance. However, Stress Tolerance is one of the most commonly found strengths in IT executives. This means that high-performing employees and managers would be much more comfortable with set schedules and well-defined tasks. They may not perform well in a crisis situation.

IT executives, on the other hand, would likely remain steady under even the most intense pressure and view daunting obstacles as welcomed challenges to overcome.

So, working together, the high performers could easily handle the pressure or criticism from other quarters while shielding the managers and employees from it. This is a good example of how Executive Skills strengths can work in combination in a team environment.

MOST FREQUENTLY FOUND EXECUTIVE SKILLS STRENGTHS: INFORMATION TECHNOLOGY

Employees	Managers	Executives
Metacognition	Planning/Prioritization	Metacognition
Working Memory	Response Inhibition	Stress Tolerance
Planning/ Prioritization	Flexibility	Working Memory

MOST FREQUENTLY FOUND EXECUTIVE SKILLS WEAKNESSES: INFORMATION TECHNOLOGY

Employees	Managers	Executives
Stress Tolerance	Stress Tolerance	Task Initiation
Task Initiation	Task Initiation	Time Management
Flexibility	Time Management	Sustained Attention

With both employees and managers strong in Planning/Prioritization, their role could be to determine the sequence of projects and organize the flow. The executive, strong in Stress Tolerance, could manage any internal or external criticism and schedule changes or conflicts, so that the weak Stress Tolerance of the employees and managers is never taxed.

The other insight is that to help select a person for promotion into an executive position in IT, it could be useful to determine who at a lower level is strong in Stress Tolerance, since that is the skill not commonly found in high performers at a lower level. Fewer than 10 percent of high-performing IT employees and just over 10 percent of managers are strong in Stress Tolerance, but therein lies the key.

If there are several candidates for possible promotion into the executive ranks and they're all high-performing managers, it's highly unlikely they all are strong in Stress Tolerance. However, there's a chance that one of them is, since a far smaller percentage of managers are strong in Stress Tolerance than those weak in it. If you can identify the candidate who possesses that skill as a strength, there's a higher probability of that person's Executive Skills matching those of ones who already are high performers at the executive level.

This same approach can be used for considering promotions in other departments, by determining the Executive Skill strength found in high performers at the higher level and then looking for someone with that skill at the lower level. Since it's common that a significantly larger percentage of high performers at higher levels in specific departments possess the skill than those at lower levels, it can narrow the field of potential candidates. This is because, as is the case in IT managers compared to IT executives, the strength found in high-performing executives is more often a weakness in managers. However, there's still a small percentage of managers who possess it as a strength, and those are the people who have the Executive Skills more like those of current successful executives.

This approach of using Executive Skills strengths matching can eliminate much of the guesswork on who is likely or not likely to succeed in a new role or job.

Operations: Order and Organization

The picture of those who work in operations is one of being orderly and logically dealing with what's next, which is what might logically be expected from those who work in operations at various levels. This picture emerges because there are some similar Executive Skills found at each level.

High-performing employees and managers are strong in Organization, and managers and executives are strong in Planning/Prioritization, both of which would contribute to making it natural for an orderly process. All things have their place, and the priorities are clear.

Employees, managers, and executives are commonly found to be strong in Metacognition, which means that high performers at all levels in operations are likely to be highly aware of what's going on around them and are continually seeking improvement both in how they do things and in those they work with. They're the ones more likely to be first to introduce or suggest a new or potentially better way to do things. These suggestions may make sense to others, who may not be strong in Metacognition, which would not necessarily make them resistant to the new way; it's just that they're unlikely to spot it first, not being strong in Metacognition.

MOST FREQUENTLY FOUND EXECUTIVE SKILLS STRENGTHS: OPERATIONS

Employees	Managers	Executives
Organization	Flexibility	Planning/ Prioritization
Metacognition	Planning/Prioritization	Goal-Directed Persistence
Sustained Attention	Organization	Metacognition

MOST FREQUENTLY FOUND EXECUTIVE SKILLS WEAKNESSES: OPERATIONS

Employees	Managers	Executives
Stress Tolerance	Emotional Control	Task Initiation
Organization	Task Initiation	Organization
Emotional Control	Response Inhibition	Time Management

The big difference in operations, though, is that more executives are driven than those at the manager level, and significantly more executives are driven than those at the employee level. Goal-Directed Persistence is one of the most commonly found strengths in executives, a stark contrast to employees, where it's the least commonly found of all 12 strengths. This is also a finding for those at the CEO level, as discussed earlier.

As in IT, this is another area where there's an opportunity to seek out the employee or manager strong in Goal-Directed Persistence, a skill that sets apart high performers at the executive level from those at the manager or employee level. They may be harder to find, since there aren't as many of them, but they're a minority among the high performers at both the employee and manager level in operations.

Administrative: Organization Is Key

In administrative departments, Organization is king, at least until you reach the executive level, where things change. For high-performing employees and managers in administrative areas, Organization is the most frequently found strength. At the employee level, more than three of every five high performers are strong in Organization, but at the manager level, it drops to two out of every five. However, it's more critical at the employee level, since only a small percentage of employees possess it as a weakness. For managers, while it's the most commonly found strength, it's also a weakness in about the same percentage of high-performing managers, indicating that the skill isn't critical to be a high-performing manager in administrative departments.

At the executive level, Organization is even less important, with slightly more than one in ten executives being strong in Organization and slightly more than a third counting it as a weakness.

At all levels of administrative departments, critical issues aren't likely to be overlooked, since Working Memory is a commonly found skill in employees, managers, and executives. A high-performing employee with this strength would likely find it a smooth transition moving into both manager and executive positions. A high-performing manager strong in Flexibility also could be a potentially good choice for an executive position, since Flexibility is a strength in almost half of high-performing executives in administrative departments.

Weaknesses in administrative departments differ among levels, with Stress Tolerance being the most frequently found weakness at the employee level, with three out of five employees counting it as a weakness compared to about a third of managers. Executives in administrative are somewhat like executives overall in the study, with Task Initiation, Time Management, and Sustained Attention being the most frequently found weaknesses. It's likely that high performers at the executive level have someone who keeps them on schedule, since they're not naturally inclined to keep track of time very well, and external factors may necessitate that certain activities start right away.

MOST FREQUENTLY FOUND EXECUTIVE SKILLS STRENGTHS: ADMINISTRATIVE

Employees	Managers	Executives
Organization	Organization	Flexibility
Working Memory	Flexibility	Working Memory
Response Inhibition	Working Memory	Planning/ Prioritization

MOST FREQUENTLY FOUND EXECUTIVE SKILLS WEAKNESSES: ADMINISTRATIVE

Employees	Managers	Executives
Stress Tolerance	Organization	Task Initiation
Emotional Control	Stress Tolerance	Time Management
Metacognition	Response Inhibition	Sustained Attention

Customer Service: Recalling Past Solutions

The strengths of high-performing employees and high-performing managers could not be much different from each other in customer service departments.[1]

High-performing customer service employees are likely to keep things in order, recall past solutions during a trying customer engagement, or keep things on schedule. This is because they're strong in Organization, Working Memory, and Time Management.

Managers, on the other hand, are likely to be very good at determining which issues should be dealt with first, can adapt to changing situations, and can easily hold their tongue when faced with a cantankerous customer. This is because they're strong in Planning/Prioritization, Flexibility, and Response Inhibition.

This may make it somewhat more difficult to easily move just anyone from employee to manager in customer service. For example, almost half of high-performing managers are strong in Planning/Prioritization, while only one in five employees has that strength. This means that a closer screening of employees to potentially promote into customer service management may be required if you want to match the Executive Skills of high-performing managers.

And like the strengths found, the weaknesses of employees and managers are mostly different from each other, the exception being that both are weak in Stress Tolerance. Though one of the strengths of employees is Organization, it's also the third most commonly found weakness in that group. This could mean either that Organization isn't a critical skill for high-performing employees or that Working Memory or Time Management is just as critical, since an employee could be strong in Working Memory while being weak in Organization. It would make sense that someone strong in either Organization or Working Memory could be a high performer, since the two skills are typical combinations, as discussed earlier. Of all high-performing employees, only a very few are strong in both Organization and Working Memory; they're typically either strong in one or the other.

MOST FREQUENTLY FOUND EXECUTIVE SKILLS STRENGTHS: CUSTOMER SERVICE

Employees	Managers
Organization	Planning/Prioritization
Working Memory	Flexibility
Time Management	Response Inhibition

MOST FREQUENTLY FOUND EXECUTIVE SKILLS WEAKNESSES: CUSTOMER SERVICE

Employees	Managers
Stress Tolerance	Task Initiation
Emotional Control	Organization
Organization	Stress Tolerance

Can Performance Be Predicted?

While no one really knows if high performance of a person in a particular job or function can be 100 percent accurately predicted before it occurs, we believe you can increase the chances of success, just as we've identified specific Executive Skills in high performers based on rank within departments.

As a side note, we looked at the Executive Skills characteristics of some college students over the course of two years in eight different classes and later compared the results against high-performing individuals in business.[2] We found that there was a pattern over the different classes over the two years. Common strengths over the classes were Organization, Working Memory, Flexibility, and Planning/Prioritization. The most commonly found strengths in our study of high performers were Working Memory, Planning/Prioritization, and Organization, all of which matched those found in the students.

Across the classes, common weak skills were Task Initiation, Sustained Attention, Emotional Control, and Stress Tolerance, the same weaknesses found most frequently in high performers.

In seven of the eight classes, the most commonly found strength was Organization, and in all of the classes, the number-one weakness was Task Initiation. In a comparison of these two Executive Skills, strengths and weaknesses across all high performers in the study, the departments where high-performing individuals with those skills were most frequently found were general management, marketing/promotion/advertising, creative/design, and sales. Many of the students seek jobs and careers in marketing/promotion/advertising, a leading area where the Executive Skills of high performers match those of the students.

This pattern is similar to the one in high performers based on where they worked, titles they held, and industries in which they resided. This begs the question, If many high performers share the same strengths, can you predict that someone moving into that position with the same strengths will succeed? We believe you can.

▪ ▪ ▪

You now have a new tool to help identify which Executive Skills are most frequently found in high performers at different levels within departments. As you can see, not all characteristics are the same based on a level within an organization. Next you'll see how you can find where people work based on each Executive Skills strength.

9

Determine Your Fit—
the High-Performance
Executive Skills Map
Where Do High Performers
with Your Strengths Work?

YOU'VE SEEN HOW to find high performers by industry, department, and job function, but there's also a way to see them from a reverse perspective, based on their strengths. By doing this, you can take your strengths and see where high performers with those same strengths work. By going through what we call the High-Performance Executive Skills Map later in this chapter), you can quickly take your top strengths and see where high performers with those same characteristics work, strength by strength. The listings allow you to map your strengths to those of high performers to see what industries, departments, and jobs they work in.

This will allow you to map any Executive Skills strengths of a colleague, subordinate, or peer as well to see where high performers with those strengths reside at work, by industry, department, and title.

There are typically two times the number of high performers in the top industry where they're found compared to the industry where the fewest work. For example, of all high-performing individuals strong in Task Initiation, two times more work in retail than in nonprofits.

This doesn't mean that everyone strong in Task Initiation should work in retail, but rather that of all those strong in Task Initiation, more work in retail than any other department, followed by healthcare, transportation, etc. It means that a high-performing individual strong in Task Initiation has a higher probability of being in retail than in the other departments. It also doesn't mean that a person strong in that skill can't succeed in nonprofits, just that there are a lot fewer of them than in retail, so the chances are lower.

The percentage of high performers working in certain departments is more pronounced with some Executive Skills than others.[1] For example, of all those strong in Response Inhibition, there's a relatively even spread of high performers across all 12 departments. But with Task Initiation, more than three times more high performers are in clinical departments than in general management. And with Time Management, there are about three times more high performers in customer service than in finance.

By job function or title, the differences in titles held based on each Executive Skill are much more pronounced than when comparing by industry or department. For example, of all high performers strong in Goal-Directed Persistence, more than a third hold the title of CEO or CFO. Of all high performers strong in Time Management, a quarter of them are employees and none hold the title of CFO. For this part of the Executive Skills Map, we select the eight most frequently held titles by high performers based on their strengths in each Executive Skill.

To create the Executive Skills Map, we analyzed each of the 12 Executive Skills strengths and matched each one to the industry and departments in which high performers work, as well as the titles they hold.[2] We believe this to be the largest known collection of high performers ranked by which percentage possesses which Executive Skills matched to the specific areas in which they work.

Following are, in order, the leading three industries and departments where high performers possessing each skill are found. In general, the first five departments comprise about half of all high performers with that particular Executive Skill. We also list the leading titles of high performers strong in each skill. (In the lists at the end of the chapter are all 10 industries, 12 departments, and 8 titles of all high performers based on each of the Executive Skills.)

Response Inhibition: Having the Capacity to Think Before Speaking or Acting

More than a third of high performers strong in Response Inhibition work in the hospitality industry, business services, or education, which includes educational services, universities, and colleges. The fewest work in technology or manufacturing. Response Inhibition is also the Executive Skill with the most balance across all departments. In the leading departments below, about one in ten high performers work in each. The departments that the fewest high performers strong in Response Inhibition work in are research and development, marketing, and sales.

The job functions or titles of those strong in Response Inhibition range from chairman/owner/partner at the top to CEO at the bottom. This does not mean a CEO can't be strong in Response Inhibition, but of all high performers strong in Response Inhibition, CEOs represent the smallest percentage.

LEADING INDUSTRIES, DEPARTMENTS, AND TITLES: RESPONSE INHIBITION

Industry	Department	Title
Hospitality	Human Resource	Chairman/ Owner/Partner
Business Services	Finance	Employee
Education	Clinical	Manager

Working Memory: The Ability to Hold Information in Memory While Performing Complex Tasks

Of all high performers strong in Working Memory, the industries where more than a third of them work are hospitality, nonprofits, or government, which includes military and public administration. And of all these high performers, about a third are found in either sales, finance, or accounting departments. The departments with the fewest are research and development and customer service.

More than 40 percent of those strong in Working Memory are CFOs, consultants, or CEOs. While the fewest of those strong in Working Memory are a manager or an employee, the spread across all eight titles is relatively even, after the first three titles.

LEADING INDUSTRIES, DEPARTMENTS, AND TITLES: WORKING MEMORY

Industry	Department	Title
Hospitality	Sales	CFO
Nonprofit, Charity	Finance	Consultant
Government	Accounting	CEO

Emotional Control: The Ability to Manage Emotions in Order to Achieve Goals, Complete Tasks, or Control and Direct Behavior

By industry, of all high-performing individuals strong in Emotional Control, more than a third work in education, manufacturing, or marketing, which includes advertising and promotion. By department, about a third are in research and development, human resources, or finance. There are more than two times the number of high performers strong in Emotional Control in research and development than in either marketing or accounting, the departments where the fewest reside.

Of all high performers strong in Emotional Control, almost half are consultants, chairmen/owners/partners, or directors. The titles held least by all of those strong in Emotional Control are CFO and CEO. Of all high performers strong in Emotional Control, there are almost two times more consultants than there are chief financial officers.

LEADING INDUSTRIES, DEPARTMENTS, AND TITLES: EMOTIONAL CONTROL

Industry	Department	Title
Education	Research and Development	Consultant
Manufacturing	Human Resources	Chairman/ Owner/Partner
Marketing	Finance	Director

Sustained Attention: The Capacity to Maintain Attention to a Situation or Task

Of all high performers strong in Sustained Attention, more than a third again are within three industries: hospitality; marketing; or transportation, which includes utilities. By department, a third work in either clinical, customer service, or administrative. The fewest of them work in marketing, which is not likely to surprise many in marketing, nor general management, with only half as many working in those departments as in clinical.

Of all high performers strong in Sustained Attention, about half are consultants, CFOs, or employees. The title held least by those strong in Sustained Attention is CEO, almost three times fewer the number of those who are consultants.

LEADING INDUSTRIES, DEPARTMENTS, AND TITLES: SUSTAINED ATTENTION

Industry	Department	Title
Hospitality	Clinical	Consultant
Marketing	Customer Service	CFO
Transportation	Administrative	Employee

Task Initiation: The Ability to Begin Tasks or Projects Without Procrastinating

You may recall that Task Initiation was a commonly found weakness among many high performers. However, there are also a number of high performers who count it as a strength, though not one of the most commonly found. Of all those who are strong in Task Initiation, the industries in which more of them work are retail, healthcare (includes medical and dental), and transportation (includes utilities).

More than a third of these high performers are in either clinical, administrative, or customer service departments, the same leading departments where those strong in Sustained Attention are found. The fewest of these high performers work in general management or sales, with three times more of them in clinical departments than in general management.

By job function, a third are either an employee or a consultant, three times more than are chairman/owner/partner and two times more than CFO, the two titles least held by those strong in Task Initiation.

LEADING INDUSTRIES, DEPARTMENTS, AND TITLES: TASK INITIATION

Industry	Department	Title
Retail	Clinical	Employee
Healthcare	Administrative	Consultant
Transportation	Customer Service	Manager

Planning/Prioritization: The Ability to Create a Road Map to Reach a Goal

Of all high performers strong in Planning/Prioritization, the top industry in which they work is technology, followed by business services and retail. Well over a third of them work in accounting, operations, systems/IT, or general management. The fewest of these high performers reside in administrative, research and development, or customer service departments.

Four of every ten high performers strong in Planning/Prioritization are CFOs, executive or senior vice presidents, or CEOs. The titles that the fewest of these high performers hold are employee or chairman/owner/partner.

LEADING INDUSTRIES, DEPARTMENTS, AND TITLES: PLANNING/PRIORITIZATION

Industry	Department	Title
Technology	Accounting	CFO
Business Services	Operations	EVP/SVP
Retail	Systems/IT	CEO

Organization: The Ability to Arrange According to a System

Of all those who are strong in Organization, the industries where more of them work are business services, transportation, or hospitality. By department, more of these high performers are found in accounting, clinical, and administrative. In fact, there are twice as many in accounting than in research and development or systems/IT.

Almost half of high performers strong in Organization are employees, consultants, or managers. The fewest of these high performers are executive or senior vice presidents, where only half as many are found as employees.

LEADING INDUSTRIES, DEPARTMENTS, AND TITLES: ORGANIZATION

Industry	Department	Title
Business Services	Accounting	Employee
Transportation	Clinical	Consultant
Hospitality	Administrative	Manager

Time Management: The Capacity to Estimate How Much Time One Has, to Allocate It, and to Stay Within Time Limitsand Deadlines

Time Management is another skill that is not found as a strength in a relatively large number of high performers overall and is a weakness in many of them. So of those who are strong in it, where they fall is somewhat more pronounced than some of the other Executive Skills.

For example, nearly half of high performers strong in Time Management work in food services, retail, or healthcare (includes medical and dental). The fewest of them work in nonprofits or manufacturing, with three times more of them in food services than in those two industries. These high performers are found more in customer service, human resources, and clinical than in any other departments. The fewest of them are in finance or sales, with three times more in customer service than in finance.

Of all high performers strong in Time Management, there is a significant spread by titles they hold. A quarter of them are at the employee level, followed by manager and chairman/owner/partner. About six out of every ten high performers strong in Time Management have one of these three titles. At the other end of the spectrum, there are no CFOs who are strong in Time Management, followed by consultants.

LEADING INDUSTRIES, DEPARTMENTS, AND TITLES: TIME MANAGEMENT

Industry	Department	Title
Food Services	Customer Service	Employee
Retail	Human Resources	Manager
Healthcare	Clinical	Chairman/ Owner/Partner

Goal-Directed Persistence: The Capacity to Have a Goal and Follow Through with Actions to Achieve It

High performers strong in Goal-Directed Persistence are more likely to work in associations, financial (includes real estate and insurance), or non-profits (includes charities). They are much less likely to be found in health-care, where there are half as many as in associations, or hospitality or retail.

As to departments, they're likely to be found in sales, general management, or marketing (includes advertising and promotion). They're much less likely to be found working in administrative or customer service departments.

The titles of high performers strong in Goal-Directed Persistence are very pronounced. Of all high performers in our study who are strong in this Executive Skill, 35 percent of them are either CFOs or CEOs. The titles with the fewest high performers strong in Goal-Directed Persistence are employee and manager.

LEADING INDUSTRIES, DEPARTMENTS, AND TITLES: GOAL-DIRECTED PERSISTENCE

Industry	Department	Title
Association	Sales	CFO
Financial Services	General Management	CEO
Nonprofit	Marketing	Director

Flexibility: The Ability to Revise Plans, Relating to the Amount of Adaptability One Has to Changing Conditions

When it comes to high performers who are strong in Flexibility, the leading industries where they reside are marketing (includes advertising and promotion), government (includes military and public administration), and technology. The fewest of these high performers are in hospitality and healthcare industries.

By department, more high performers strong in Flexibility are found in administrative departments, followed by customer service and marketing (includes advertising and promotion). The fewest of them are in clinical or accounting departments, with only half as many in clinical as in administrative, the leading department.

Those strong in Flexibility are relatively evenly spread across titles, with more being chairmen/owners/partners, executive or senior vice presidents, or managers. The fewest of them are consultants or CFOs.

LEADING INDUSTRIES, DEPARTMENTS, AND TITLES: FLEXIBILITY

Industry	Department	Title
Marketing	Administrative	Chairman/Owner/Partner
Government	Customer Service	EVP/SVP
Technology	Marketing	Manager

Metacognition: The Ability to Stand Back and Take a Bird's-Eye View of Yourself in a Situation and Be Able to Understand and Make Changes in How You Solve Problems

The industries where more high performers strong in Metacognition work are associations, manufacturing, or business services, with well over a third in those three industries. The fewest of them are in healthcare or nonprofits.

The leading departments where they work are research and development, marketing (includes advertising and promotion), and general management. The fewest of them can be found in clinical or finance industries.

About a third of high performers strong in Metacognition hold the title of chairman/owner/partner or executive or senior vice president. The fewest of them hold titles of consultant or employee.

LEADING INDUSTRIES, DEPARTMENTS, AND TITLES: METACOGNITION

Industry	Department	Title
Association	Research and Development	Chairman/Owner/Partner
Manufacturing	Marketing	EVP/SVP
Business Services	General Management	Director

Stress Tolerance: The Ability to Thrive in Stressful Situations and to Cope with Uncertainty, Change, and Performance Demands

The leading areas where those strong in Stress Tolerance are found are government (includes military and public administration), food services, and business services. The fewest of them are in healthcare or hospitality industries.

By department, more of these high performers are in operations, systems/IT, or sales than any other. The fewest are in accounting, more than two times fewer than those in operations, or clinical.

If stress flows up, this could be an indication that there are some there prepared to handle it. Of all high performers strong in Stress Tolerance, more than a third hold the titles of executive/senior vice president or CEO. The titles with the lowest number of those who are strong in that skill are chairman/owner/partner or employee, each with half as many as those with the title of executive or senior vice president.

LEADING INDUSTRIES, DEPARTMENTS, AND TITLES: STRESS TOLERANCE

Industry	Department	Title
Government	Operations	EVP/SVP
Food Services	Systems/IT	CEO
Business Services	Sales	Director

Following is the detailed breakdown of each of the 12 Executive Skills and where high performers work based on how many are strong in each skill. The details are by industry, department, and then title, based on all high performers possessing each specific skill.

The High-Performance Executive Skills Map

INDUSTRIES BY EXECUTIVE SKILLS STRENGTHS

High Response Inhibition

Hospitality 12.45%

Business Services 11.97%

Educational Svc./University/College 10.82%

Medical/Dental/Healthcare 10.62%

Nonprofit/Charity 9.58%

Financial/Real Estate/Insurance 9.34%

Government/Military/Public Adm. 9.24%

Retail 9.24%

Manufacturing 9.02%

Technology 7.72%

High Working Memory

Hospitality 12.38%

Nonprofit/Charity 11.46%

Government/Military/Public Adm. 11.24%

Medical/Dental/Healthcare 10.86%

Business Services 10.43%

Technology 9.59%

Financial/Real Estate/Insurance 9.46%

Retail 9.33%

Manufacturing 8.39%

Educational Svc./University/College 6.86%

High Emotional Control

Educational Svc./University/College 12.11%

Manufacturing 12.06%

Advertising/Marketing/Promotion 11.97%

Nonprofit/Charity 11.45%

Government/Military/Public Adm. 10.46%

Medical/Dental/Healthcare 9.18%

Business Services 8.82%

Hospitality 8.62%

Financial/Real Estate/Insurance 6.85%
Technology 6.85%

High Sustained Attention

Hospitality 11.73%
Advertising/Marketing/Promotion 11.30%
Transportation/Utilities 11.23%
Retail 10.88%
Educational Svc./University/College 10.46%
Technology 10.38%
Medical/Dental/Healthcare 9.83%
Nonprofit/Charity 8.90%
Financial/Real Estate/Insurance 7.76%
Manufacturing 7.53%

High Task Initiation

Retail 14.07%
Medical/Dental/Healthcare 12.10%
Transportation/Utilities 11.50%
Educational Svc./University/College 10.67%
Hospitality 10.48%
Financial/Real Estate/Insurance 9.57%
Manufacturing 8.63%
Government/Military/Public Adm. 8.09%
Technology 7.61%
Nonprofit/Charity 7.29%

High Planning/Prioritization

Technology 12.00%
Business Services 11.24%
Retail 11.12%
Medical/Dental/Healthcare 10.66%
Government/Military/Public Adm. 10.38%
Manufacturing 10.05%
Nonprofit/Charity 9.30%
Educational Svc./University/College 9.12%

Financial/Real Estate/Insurance 8.41%
Hospitality 7.72%

High Organization

Business Services 12.03%
Transportation/Utilities 11.54%
Hospitality 10.67%
Retail 10.42%
Medical/Dental/Healthcare 10.37%
Nonprofit/Charity 9.41%
Technology 9.14%
Financial/Real Estate/Insurance 9.02%
Manufacturing 8.84%
Educational Svc./University/College 8.55%

High Time Management

Food Services 17.55%
Retail 14.55%
Medical/Dental/Healthcare 12.10%
Hospitality 11.36%
Educational Svc./University/College 8.81%
Technology 7.85%
Government/Military/Public Adm. 7.52%
Financial/Real Estate/Insurance 7.24%
Manufacturing 6.55%
Nonprofit/Charity 6.47%

High Goal-Directed Persistence

Association 13.39%
Financial/Real Estate/Insurance 11.98%
Nonprofit/Charity 11.10%
Technology 10.71%
Manufacturing 10.06%
Government/Military/Public Adm. 9.49%
Educational Svc./University/College 9.01%
Retail 8.40%

Hospitality 8.17%
Medical/Dental/Healthcare 7.70%

High Flexibility

Advertising/Marketing/Promotion 12.92%
Government/Military/Public Adm. 11.72%
Technology 10.56%
Manufacturing 10.52%
Financial/Real Estate/Insurance 10.41%
Educational Svc./University/College 9.98%
Nonprofit/Charity 9.45%
Business Services 9.06%
Medical/Dental/Healthcare 7.90%
Hospitality 7.47%

High Metacognition

Association 14.65%
Manufacturing 11.04%
Business Services 10.86%
Financial/Real Estate/Insurance 10.36%
Retail 9.71%
Educational Svc./University/College 9.43%
Government/Military/Public Adm. 9.11%
Technology 8.97%
Nonprofit/Charity 8.95%
Medical/Dental/Healthcare 6.91%

High Stress Tolerance

Government/Military/Public Adm. 13.05%
Food Services 12.12%
Business Services 11.53%
Educational Svc./University/College 10.24%
Technology 10.22%
Financial/Real Estate/Insurance 10.05%
Manufacturing 9.56%
Nonprofit/Charity 8.55%

Hospitality 7.92%
Medical/Dental/Healthcare 6.75%

DEPARTMENTS BY EXECUTIVE SKILLS STRENGTHS

High Response Inhibition

Human Resources 9.98%
Finance 9.77%
Clinical 9.23%
Systems/IT 9.21%
Administrative 9.08%
Operations 8.07%
Customer Service 8.02%
Accounting 7.76%
General Management 7.62%
Sales 7.58%
Marketing/Promotion/Advertising 7.49%
Research & Development 6.19%

High Working Memory

Sales 10.53%
Finance 10.45%
Accounting 9.23%
Marketing/Promotion/Advertising 9.22%
Human Resources 9.06%
General Management 8.61%
Administrative 8.04%
Operations 7.38%
Systems/IT 7.31%
Clinical 7.12%
Customer Service 6.74%
Research & Development 6.31%

High Emotional Control

Research & Development 11.51%
Human Resources 9.84%
Finance 9.78%

Systems/IT 8.85%
Administrative 8.65%
General Management 8.50%
Clinical 8.39%
Customer Service 8.39%
Operations 7.66%
Sales 6.69%
Accounting 6.08%
Marketing/Promotion/Advertising 5.66%

High Sustained Attention
Clinical 11.10%
Customer Service 10.74%
Administrative 10.32%
Accounting 10.19%
Finance 9.92%
Systems/IT 9.59%
Sales 9.10%
Research & Development 8.60%
Operations 8.41%
General Management 6.03%
Marketing/Promotion/Advertising 5.99%

High Task Initiation
Clinical 13.16%
Administrative 11.33%
Customer Service 11.05%
Accounting 8.32%
Human Resources 8.17%
Research & Development 7.97%
Finance 7.73%
Operations 7.46%
Systems/IT 7.27%
Marketing/Promotion/Advertising 7.00%
Sales 6.44%
General Management 4.09%

High Planning/Prioritization

Accounting 10.41%
Operations 9.42%
Systems/IT 9.31%
General Management 9.19%
Clinical 9.04%
Marketing/Promotion/Advertising 8.56%
Sales 7.95%
Human Resources 7.87%
Finance 7.65%
Customer Service 7.56%
Research & Development 7.01%
Administrative 6.02%

High Organization

Accounting 11.89%
Clinical 9.96%
Administrative 9.38%
Customer Service 8.93%
Human Resources 8.56%
General Management 7.91%
Marketing/Promotion/Advertising 7.90%
Finance 7.90%
Operations 7.50%
Sales 6.99%
Systems/IT 6.68%
Research & Development 6.42%

High Time Management

Customer Service 13.27%
Human Resources 12.61%
Clinical 11.56%
Administrative 8.92%
Accounting 8.66%
Research & Development 8.20%
Systems/IT 7.76%

Operations 6.62%
Marketing/Promotion/Advertising 6.31%
General Management 5.89%
Sales 5.56%
Finance 4.64%

High Goal-Directed Persistence

Sales 12.13%
General Management 12.00%
Marketing/Promotion/Advertising 10.38%
Research & Development 9.67%
Operations 9.66%
Accounting 9.44%
Finance 8.59%
Clinical 7.94%
Systems/IT 7.91%
Customer Service 6.26%
Administrative 6.02%

High Flexibility

Administrative 10.17%
Customer Service 9.88%
Marketing/Promotion/Advertising 9.51%
Finance 8.95%
Operations 8.81%
Sales 8.55%
Systems/IT 8.42%
General Management 8.27%
Research & Development 8.00%
Human Resources 7.46%
Accounting 6.03%
Clinical 5.09%

High Metacognition

Research & Development 12.49%
Marketing/Promotion/Advertising 10.50%

General Management 10.30%
Human Resources 9.61%
Systems/IT 9.19%
Operations 8.81%
Sales 8.47%
Administrative 6.91%
Accounting 6.43%
Customer Service 6.29%
Finance 5.90%
Clinical 5.09%

High Sress Tolerance

Operations 10.63%
Systems/IT 10.08%
Sales 9.59%
Research & Development 9.59%
General Management 9.43%
Marketing/Promotion/Advertising 9.29%
Finance 8.59%
Administrative 7.95%
Customer Service 7.59%
Human Resources 7.10%
Clinical 6.01%
Accounting 4.15%

JOB FUNCTIONS/TITLES BY EXECUTIVE SKILLS STRENGTHS

High Response Inhibition

Chairman/Owner/Partner 16.50%
Employee 14.04%
Manager 13.65%
Director 12.90%
CFO 12.87%
Consultant 11.93%
EVP/SVP 10.42%
CEO 7.68%

High Working Memory

CFO 14.34%

Consultant 13.93%

CEO 13.53%

Director 12.26%

EVP/SVP 12.16%

Chairman/Owner/Partner 11.61%

Employee 11.59%

Manager 10.59%

High Emotional Control

Consultant 16.81%

Chairman/Owner/Partner 14.67%

Director 13.63%

Manager 12.33%

Employee 12.01%

EVP/SVP 11.46%

CEO 10.03%

CFO 9.06%

High Sustained Attention

Consultant 16.67%

CFO 15.22%

Employee 15.13%

Chairman/Owner/Partner 12.32%

Manager 12.06%

EVP/SVP 11.76%

Director 10.43%

CEO 6.41%

High Task Initiation

Employee 18.96%

Consultant 16.76%

Manager 13.18%

CEO 13.16%

Director 10.80%

EVP/SVP 10.64%
CFO 9.86%
Chairman/Owner/Partner 6.65%

High Planning Prioritization
CFO 14.53%
EVP/SVP 14.12%
CEO 12.86%
Consultant 12.80%
Manager 12.45%
Director 11.54%
Chairman/Owner/Partner 11.18%
Employee 10.52%

High Organization
Employee 16.61%
Consultant 14.97%
Manager 13.89%
CFO 13.59%
CEO 11.82%
Director 10.90%
Chairman/Owner/Partner 9.63%
EVP/SVP 8.60%

High Time Management
Employee 25.34%
Manager 18.01%
Chairman/Owner/Partner 15.12%
CEO 11.81%
EVP/SVP 11.34%
Director 9.73%
Consultant 8.66%
CFO 0%

High Goal-Directed Persistence
CFO 17.72%
CEO 17.21%

Director 13.84%
Consultant 12.14%
EVP/SVP 10.60%
Chairman/Owner/Partner 10.60%
Manager 10.40%
Employee 7.50%

High Flexibility
Chairman/Owner/Partner 14.56%
EVP/SVP 14.21%
Manager 13.61%
Director 13.46%
CEO 13.36%
Employee 10.99%
CFO 10.28%
Consultant 9.53%

High Metacognition
Chairman/Owner/Partner 17.31%
EVP/SVP 14.42%
Director 13.84%
Manager 12.95%
CEO 12.35%
CFO 11.08%
Employee 10.71%
Consultant 7.34%

High Stress Tolerance
EVP/SVP 18.61%
CEO 16.23%
Director 13.72%
Consultant 10.91%
Manager 10.73%
CFO 10.69%
Employee 9.58%
Chairman/Owner/Partner 9.52%

Now you see how you can note your own Executive Skills strengths and weaknesses and see where high performers with the same skills as you work. This can give you an idea of where you have a higher probability of becoming a high performer. This also provides an indicator of where you *may* not be a good fit, where your key weaknesses correlate to the strengths most frequently found in certain positions, so these could be areas for you to avoid.

And if by chance you already are in a position where your skills are an obvious mismatch, at least you now know why and can devise strategies to find a better fit, which we discuss in the next and final chapter.

Conclusion

SIMPLY KNOWING about Executive Skills strengths and weaknesses in yourself and others is useful only if you do something about it. If you've read this entire book (if you're strong in Sustained Attention, it would have been easier; if you're weak in Task Initiation, it was likely a while before you started and got to this chapter), you understand strengths and weaknesses and how they're found in successful people in all types of jobs, departments, and industries. You can tell where they are.

Executive Skills are a real thing, not a theory or speculation about how people might behave when executing or performing certain tasks. Once you come to terms with this fact, it becomes easier to understand and anticipate behaviors in work situations. Linking your new knowledge to the strengths of high performers based on where they work and what they do becomes a powerful tool for personal planning and for jobs and career moves.

For example, you're in a good situation if you determine that one or more of your top three strengths is among those most required for the job you have. On the other hand, if you're in a position that not only doesn't play to your strengths, but also plays to your weakest Executive Skills, you're in a situation where you have many effortful tasks and, hence, may not be in the best situation.

It's obviously not practical to leave your job right away just because your strengths don't match the job. However, there are specific steps you can take to ensure that going forward you end up with more goodness-of-fit situations and fewer effortful task situations for yourself. There are steps you can take on the road to high performance.

Determine your strengths and weaknesses. The first thing is to measure your own strengths and weaknesses. The results are neither good nor bad, since everyone has Executive Skills strengths and weaknesses. It's knowing what they are that gives you the insight on how to best leverage what you're likely to be good at. What are your two or three strongest skills and your two or three weakest?

Assess strengths and weaknesses required for your current job. Take a look at the requirements of your current position to determine which Executive Skills are most needed on a regular basis. Do things need to get started right away? That would mean Task Initiation is most needed. Do things constantly change and require readjustment throughout your day? That would be Flexibility. Is the end game what you are really judged on? That would be Goal-Directed Persistence. Look at the behavior needed and match that to the appropriate Executive Skill.

Measure those around you. By identifying high performers in the area in which you work, you can get an idea of likely strengths needed. Is someone with a similar function performing much better than you, and if so, what are the Executive Skills that go with that performance? You can see if these are the same or different strengths from the ones you have. You can do this the other way as well. If you're a high performer and people around you with similar job functions are not, they probably have a different set of strengths than you.

Determine your current fit. Once you can tell who the high performers are, of which you may be one, you can see how you fit in the entire situation. This gives you a benchmark and shows the strengths of high performance in context in relation to yourself. For example, you can tell if there are few high performers and if their strengths are the same. How do your strengths match in your current role as well as your potential next role, such as in the next logical assignment or promotion?

Determine potential fits. Observe the behaviors of high performers in areas you seek to move to, whether in a different department or as part of the next logical career move, perhaps a promotion. Determine where your strengths most come into play. Use the tables in this book to see where your strengths are a likely fit and strive toward those positions. This approach can also help you avoid moving to a position that's a mismatch between your strengths and those required for the job.

Suggest to others what you're good at. Promote to others the behaviors that play to your strengths because others may not be familiar with Executive Skills or recognize the inherent strengths you bring to the table. If you're strong in Time Management, offer to manage the time aspects of a meeting or project. This will be easy for you. It's okay to say, "I'm pretty good at managing time, so why don't I take a crack at determining how long this will take?" Those weak in Time Management will appreciate this. If you're strong in Task Initiation, suggest that you take the lead in starting a project after a meeting or taking the first steps in a team situation. That will be very natural for you.

Make the right move at the right time. Watch for upcoming openings that you know play to your strengths. You can use the tables in the book to match where you're likely to be a high performer as well as your own observations within your organization. By identifying your potential best fits in advance, you can better plan and focus on next moves, whether internal or external. If, for whatever reason, you're not working, this knowledge can provide you with a potential career switch to something that's a perfect fit with your Executive Skills.

Our intent is for this knowledge to help you throughout your work life, from day-to-day interactions with others to long-term career planning. And if you manage others, it should help you determine the right person for the right seat when one becomes open. We hope this book, by looking at where certain Executive Skills are found in successful businesspeople at all levels, can help you work your strengths on your own personal road to high performance.

APPENDIXES

How the Two-Year Study Was Conducted
High Performers and the Executive Skills Profile

Over the course of two years, we contacted organizations of every size and type to invite them to participate in our "study to determine the cognitive characteristics of high-performing individuals in business." We typically sent a detailed invitation to an executive; a department head; a manager; an HR department; or, in many cases, the CEO. We wanted to directly contact the people who could most easily identify high-performing individuals in their department or organization. Most organizations agreed to participate because we offered to share each organization's aggregate results of its high performers with the organization. All surveys were totally anonymous, so we didn't capture or record any participants' names or e-mail addresses, other than those of the person we contacted.

We ultimately concluded that the manager, executive, or department head would be best positioned to determine the particular criteria for his or her high performers and that there would likely be differences based on each situation, which somewhat turned out to be the case, though most of the criteria fell within a specific range of reasons.

Interestingly, though the high-performing selection criteria varied widely from business to business, there was never any doubt that the manager or executive knew exactly who his or her high performers were. There were no cases in the study where a manager, an executive, or a business leader could not readily identify his or her high performers. During the early months of the study, when we would ask people how many high performers they could identify in their area, managers would typically think for a few seconds, as if visually counting their high performers, and then tell us the number. One of the reasons that executives and managers could so quickly and easily identify their high performers for our study could be that, in general, the majority of employees are not high performers.

It also turned out that not all parts of the same organization determine their high performers the same way. For example, two divisions in one company used slightly different criteria to select their high performers. While one department identified its high performers by "quality of work, efficiency, and success within the company," another used "length of employment, proven job history, and strong customer service skills." Despite the somewhat different criteria for selection, it turned out that the majority of high performers from each of the two divisions had strikingly similar combinations of Executive Skills strengths and weaknesses.

In some cases, our contact would tell us how many high performers he or she could identify in the organization, and we would mail that number of surveys to the contact. That person would then distribute the questionnaire to his or her high performers, collect all the results, and forward them back to us for tabulation. We mailed thousands of surveys to these businesses around the United States and Canada. In other cases, we created online links for organizations to participate. Each link was unique, so data were returned to a location at NFI Research that identified the company or organization name but left those surveys totally anonymous. These links were sent to hundreds of organizations in and outside the United States. These links are still being sent, as we continue to increase the size of the high performers' database.

We surveyed high-performing individuals across industries, job functions, and organization sizes. We surveyed people at Fortune 500 companies, small companies, nonprofit organizations, hospitals, financial institutions, manufacturing businesses, retailers, and many other categories, as well as multiple departments and job functions and titles.

For the first several months, we tested the questionnaire with select executives we knew in different categories of organizations. We wanted to determine how long the questionnaires took for individuals, the return time, and the return rate. We also slightly modified some of the wording and increased the number of categories based on early feedback. In the test, we quickly saw patterns in the areas of organizations that completed profiles.

By the time we received 800 completed surveys, the overall data had stabilized, which meant that when we received another hundred and another hundred, the total numbers increased but the percentages remained the same. We continued the process past 2,500 completed surveys so that we could include more segments in the final results and conduct more detailed comparisons.

DETERMINING HIGH PERFORMANCE

Because there was no way we could determine who the high-performing individuals were in so many organizations, we delegated that to the contact at the organization. Each person we contacted typically knew right away how many high performers he or she could identify. For the study, we asked each participant to tell us the criteria he or she used, which we detailed in an earlier chapter. Some of the criteria were similar and quantitative; others were somewhat more subjective, as we also detailed earlier in the book.

The high performers selected by the executive or department head were not necessarily told they were selected for the study because they were high performers; they were just asked to complete a survey. There was no mention on the survey itself of it being sent only to high performers unless the executive forwarding it told them.

In discussing the study with a group of executives, several asked if we could determine who the low performers were because those were the people they wanted to identify early. However, we did not attempt to do that and focused only on high-performing individuals. If there was doubt as to a potential participant being a high performer, such as a volunteer who wanted to participate because he or she heard of the study by word of mouth, we typically did not include that person's results.

USING THE EXECUTIVE SKILLS PROFILE

To determine the Executive Skills of the high performers, we used our Executive Skills Profile, which we retitled *Executive Skills Survey* for the study. It is the same instrument we have used in the business marketplace for several years and the instrument used to profile attendees at SMARTS seminars as well as many other individuals over the years.[1] It is also featured in our previous book, *SMARTS: Are We Hardwired for Success?*

The profile comprises a total of 60 questions, with five addressing each of the 12 Executive Skills (see The Questionnaire later in this chapter). The 60 questions are random in the profile, both in print and in the electronic version. Each participant was asked to answer the questions with a range of how much he or she agreed or disagreed with a statement based on a scale of one to four.

Over the course of the study, more than 2,500, sixty-question surveys were answered, for a total of more than 150,000 individual questions answered.

After tabulation, we selected each participant's three strongest and three weakest Executive Skills. In case of a tie for, say, the third skill, we used a randomization program to select from the tied answers. In most cases, the top strengths and weaknesses were very clear and the high performers typically had two or three in each case, with the remaining skills falling somewhere in between. This has been a common experience of all of the authors, with Richard Guare and Peg Dawson identifying it with patients over a period of many years in psychology and Chuck Martin identifying it over a period of several years with businesspeople.

Out of thousands of high-performing individuals who answered the questionnaire, only a very few answered high across the board. And since the surveys were anonymous, this may have been because the person just needed to quickly get through the questionnaire that he or she was asked to complete by a superior. Or, the person could have been doing a good job faking. Virtually no organizations had more than one person who answered this way.

The strengths and weaknesses of one person and another can be compared, but not the absolute scores. In our study, we found that each survey typically followed the pattern of the answers being relative to each other within that one questionnaire. For example, one person may have tended to answer questions with higher scores across the board. In those cases, the low still stood out in stark contrast to the high scores. In cases where high performers tended to answer with lower scores across the board, the highs also stood out significantly from the low scores.

In relaying the aggregate answers to study participants, not one organization disagreed with the Executive Skills strengths and weaknesses profiles of its high performers. The more respondents there were from an organization, the more distinct the profile became. For example, the majority of one large financial services company's top executives completed the profile, and we found that 63 percent of them shared the same Executive Skills strength and 56 percent of them shared the same Executive Skills weakness. More significantly, their best clients, who were attending a meeting with the executives, also completed the profiles and we found that the Executive Skills strength in the largest percentage of them was the same one as in executives from the hosting company. However, there were differences found between the two, which helped them see how to more effectively interact with each other.

SELECTING SUBJECTS

We used several sources and methods to identify and invite participants for the study. NFI Research invited its senior executive and manager members to participate, which drew a relatively large response. During the first three months, a team of 15 student researchers from the Whittemore School of Business and Economics at the University of New Hampshire (UNH) worked on the project, contacting organizations, identifying industry types, collecting results, and communicating with the businesses participating in the study. All researchers were juniors or seniors, almost all marketing majors in the business school. And because UNH students were participating, the survey methodology was submitted to the Institutional Review Board (IRB) of the university, which reviewed and approved it.

The American Management Association, the parent company of the publisher of this book, invited its members to participate. The editor-in-chief of *CIO Magazine*, a well-known and highly regarded publication targeted to chief information officers (CIOs) and other high-level information technology (IT) professionals, invited its subscribers to participate. We invited attendees at SMARTS seminars, which one of the authors (Chuck Martin) conducted within various businesses on behalf of the American Management Association.

Over the course of the study, 98 additional researchers worked with us to identify and recruit organizations of all types to participate. Over the course of two years, a total of 113 researchers worked on the study in one way or another.

Members of the research team for the study of high performing individuals.

In several cases, participants from one organization, especially the larger ones, came from more than one source. Interestingly, there rarely was an overlap situation where potential participants said they had already been contacted or had completed the questionnaire.

SELECTING INDUSTRY TYPES AND DEPARTMENTS

Planning a study for thousands of respondents, we wanted to be able to determine results from a very wide range of industries and areas where people worked. We wanted to be able to analyze results from a department and be able to look at that department by industry, and vice versa. For example, we might want to look at the characteristics of high-performing salespeople in retail compared to high-performing salespeople in food services or pharmaceuticals. Therefore, we included a large number of department categories as well as industry types.

Industry types included in the study are:

- Advertising/Marketing/
  Promotion
- Agriculture/Mining
- Association

- Business Services
- Consulting
- Educational Svc./
  University/College

- Financial/Real Estate/
  Insurance
- Food Services
- Government/Military/
  Public Adm.
- Hospitality
- Human Services
- Internet/Online Services
- Legal
- Manufacturing
- Media/Entertainment

- Medical/Dental/Healthcare
- Nonprofit/Charity
- Pharmaceuticals
- Public Relations
- Retail
- Sports
- Technology
- Telecommunications
- Transportation/Utilities
- Travel/Tourism
- Wholesale Distribution

The study includes surveys completed from virtually every category of industry type. We also included many department names, which are:

- Accounting
- Administrative
- Clinical
- Creative/Design
- Customer Service
- Finance
- General Management
- Human Resources
- Internet

- Legal
- Marketing/Promotion/
  Advertising
- Operations
- Public Relations
- Research & Development
- Sales
- Systems/IT

In the case of departments, high performers from every department listed participated in the study. The departments with the most participants were sales, general management, operations, systems/IT, advertising/marketing/promotion, administrative, customer service, finance, and accounting, each of which we profiled earlier in the book.

JOB FUNCTIONS AND TITLES

One of our goals in the study was to determine if there were any differences in Executive Skills in high performers by level in an organization. Does the

CEO have a different set of Executive Skills than the CFO? What about employee vs. manager vs. senior executive? What about sales employee vs. sales manager? What about sales employee vs. sales executive? Do any titles share the same Executive Skills weaknesses? We ultimately found the answers to all of these questions.

The study includes participants from every title we listed, which are:

- CEO
- CFO
- Chairman/Owner/Partner
- CIO
- CLO
- CMO

- Consultant
- COO
- Director
- Employee
- EVP/SVP
- Manager

HIGH PERFORMERS BY AGE AND GENDER

As far as we can determine, no one has ever measured in any significant way if there are any similarities or differences in Executive Skills between males and females or by age, especially across a group of high performers in business. Because we were capturing significant demographic information anyway, we included two questions regarding age and gender. Selections in age range were:

- 20–30
- 31–40
- 41–50
- 51–60
- 61+

The overwhelming majority of participants answered both the age and gender questions. There were only slightly more male than female participants in the overall study, and we did find one significant difference in Executive Skills between males and females. High performers in every age category participated in the study. By age, about 40 percent of respondents were between 20 and 40, and the remainder were 41 or older. About 4 percent were 61 or older. We also analyzed if there were similarities or differences in Executive Skills strengths and weaknesses in high performers by age.

HIGH PERFORMERS BY COMPANY SIZE

The study comprises high performers in organizations of all sizes. Slightly more than half of high performers in the study work at organizations with fewer than 1,000 employees. About 20 percent are from organizations with 100 or fewer employees, while almost a third work in organizations with 5,000 or more employees.

THE QUESTIONNAIRE

Following are the questionnaire items used to determine the Executive Skills strengths and weaknesses of high-performing individuals in business. More than 2,500 questionnaires were answered.

1. I typically break big tasks down into subtasks and timelines.

2. I make sure I have all the facts before I take action.

3. I am good at remembering the things that I have committed to do.

4. I seldom make comments that make people uncomfortable.

5. When I have a lot to do, I focus on the most important things.

6. I very naturally remember to complete tasks.

7. I can get right to work even if there's something I'd rather be doing.

8. I find it easy to stay focused on my work.

9. When I start my day I have a clear plan in mind for what I hope to accomplish.

10. When I'm busy, I keep track of both the big picture and the details.

11. I have formulated plans to achieve most of my important long-term goals.

12. I usually handle confrontations calmly.

13. Once I start an assignment, I work diligently until it is completed.

14. I think before I speak.

15. I easily defer my personal feelings until after a task has been completed.

16. Even when interrupted, I get back to work to complete the job at hand.

17. Procrastination is usually not a problem for me.

18. When I have a job to do or task to finish I easily avoid distractions.

19. I generally start tasks early.

20. I keep sight of goals that I want to accomplish.

21. Once I've been given a job or task, I like to start it immediately.

22. When frustrated or angry, I keep my cool.

23. I can keep my emotions in check when on the job.

24. I am good at identifying priorities and sticking to them.

25. I see myself as tactful and diplomatic.

26. I have a good memory of facts, dates, and details.

27. I attend to a task even when I find it somewhat tedious.

28. I take my time before making up my mind.

29. No matter what the task, I believe in getting started as soon as possible.

30. Little things don't affect me emotionally and distract me from the task at hand.

31. I think quickly on my feet.

32. I am good at maintaining systems for organizing my work.

33. I am usually on time for appointments and activities.

34. I like jobs where there are not many set schedules.

35. I can adjust quickly to unexpected events.

36. When I encounter an obstacle, I still achieve my goal.

37. I routinely set and follow a daily schedule of activities.

38. I am an organized person.

39. It is easy for me to keep track of my materials.

40. I consider myself to be flexible and adaptive to change.

41. I can review a situation and see where I could have done things differently.

42. I pace myself according to the time demands of a task.

43. At the end of the day, I've usually finished what I set out to do.

44. I enjoy strategic thinking and sound problem solving.

45. Jobs that include a fair degree of unpredictability appeal to me.

46. It's easy for me to organize things, such as email, inbox, and to-do items.

47. I enjoy working in a highly demanding, fast-paced environment.

48. I have a good ability to set long-term goals.

49. I easily recognize when a task is a good match for my skills and abilities.

50. I generally step back from a situation in order to make objective decisions.

51. I am good at estimating how long it takes to do something.

52. I think of myself as being driven to meet my goals.

53. I am good at setting and achieving high levels of performance.

54. I am comfortable taking risks when the situation calls for it.

55. I routinely evaluate my performance and devise methods for personal improvement.

56. Pressure helps me perform at my best.

57. I find it easy to alter my agenda to someone else's.

58. It is natural for me to keep my work area neat and organized.

59. I easily adjust to changes in plans and priorities.

60. I easily give up immediate pleasures while working on long-term goals.

ORGANIZATIONS IN THE STUDY

Following are the names of the organizations where high performers participated in the study. In some cases, there are participants from different parts of the same company and in other cases from certain divisions or departments.

211info	Air Graphics
99 Restaurant	A Little Easier Recovery
AAA	Alliance Member Services
Ablitt Law Office PC	Allstate
Acushnet Company	Alpco Diagnostics
Adams County Government	Alt Marketing
Advent Software	American Financial and Automotive Services
Aetna	
Air Force	American Management Association

American Sporting Goods

American Water

Ames Planning Associates

Amherst Label

Analog Devices

Annex Consulting Group Inc.

Anthem Blue Cross

Appledore Marine

Applied Biosystems

Arca Bipharma

Ardent Support Technologies

Armstrong Shaw Associates

Aspirus

Association of Electric Cooperatives

Assurant

Atlantic Pathology

Atrius Health Harvard Vanguard

BAE Systems

Bain & Company

Baked Beads

Bank of America

Barnstable Police Department

Bayhead Products Corporation

BDP International

BeadforLife

Bell South

Best Buy

Biblical Concourse of Home Universities

BIC Consumer Products, Inc.

Big Brothers Big Sisters of Central California

Big Hit Media

Bio San Laboratories, Inc.

Biovail Pharmaceuticals

Black & Decker

BNY Mellon

Bosch Rexroth

Boston Towing & Transportation

Boyne Resorts

Brady Sullivan Properties

Bridges Resort and Tennis Club

Brimmer and May School

Brookline Bank

Cafco Construction

California Credit Union League

Cambridge Fire Department

Campus Federal Credit Union

Cape Codder Resort and Spa

Cape Fish and Lobster Co.

Cardinal Healthcare Mexicali

Care Communications Inc.

Carlin Contracting Co.

Carlson Investment Group

Cascades

Casella Waste Management

Cendyn

Centrex Labs

Centria

Century Label, Inc.

Charles River Development

Cheshire Medical Center/Dartmouth Hitchcock Keene

Chest PT Services, Inc.

Child & Family Institute

CHS

Chunky's Cinema

Cisco

City of Stamford

CNA Insurance

Coastal Federal Credit Union

Coca-Cola

Collegiate Enterprises

Columbia Construction Company

ComEd

Commercial Resources Inc.

Community Initiatives

Concord Litho

Consolidated Brick

Consultant Jocelyn Benoit Inc.

Converge

Converse

Cooperative Benefits and Financial
Services

Coosa County Probate

Courtesy Insurance Agency

Craft Brewers Alliance (Red Hook)

C Squared Systems

CVS Pharmacy

Cytogenetics Laboratory

Data Frenzy, LLC

David Castlegrant and Associates, LLC

Deep Partners Brand Design

DePuy Spine, Inc.

Detica

Discovery Communications Group

Diversified Staffing Services

Dresser, Inc.

DryTek

Dubai Duty Free

Dunkin' Donuts

DuPont

Durham Police Department

Duxbury Student Union

EAC

Eaglebrook Engineering and Survey
LLC

E&S Technologies

Eastern Bank

eCoast Sales Solutions

Edgewater Technology

E Lanes

El Dorado Arts Council

Elliot Hospital

EMC

Energen

Enterprise Bank

Ernst & Young LLP

Esselte

Euro RSCG Edge

Exeter Health Resources Inc.

Exeter Hospital

Faxton-St. Luke's Healthcare

Feldenkrais Guild of North America

FICP Meeting Planners

FICP Suppliers

Fidelity

Filias Construction/Realty

Fireye Inc.

First Data

Flint Communications

Florida Department of Transportation

Food Recruiting

For Eyes Optical

Foundation for Affordable Housing

Galveston County Small Business
Development Center

GE

Genesis Healthcare

Glendale Elementary School

Gold Canyon

Goodman Speakers Bureau

Grainger

Grand Circle Travel

Granite Edge Consulting, LLC

Great Point Inc.

Greenberg Traurig, LLP

Griffin York and Krause

Groton Biosystems

GTECH

Hadley Media

Hampton Inn

HandsOn Central California

Hanover Insurance Group

Harper Industries, Inc.

Harris NA

Hartford Life

Harvard Pilgrim Healthcare

Harvey Building Products

Harvey Industries

Healthcare Reimbursement Specialist, Inc.

Henry A. Petter Supply Co.

Higher IT

Hill Holiday

Hillsboro-Deering School District

Hilton Boston Logan Airport

Hopkinton Middle and High Schools

Hot Stuff Foods

HP

Hrnovations

HRVP

IBM

Industrial & Commercial Security

ING

Inland Empire Credit Union

Intel

Interactive Data Corporation

Interbank

International City/County

Management Association

Interstate Hotels

Intetics Co

Investment Consulting Group, Inc.

Investors Group

IR Strategic Advisors

Island Partners Hawaii

Jackson Lumber

Jackson Safety

J & K Sales Associates

JEBCO

J.Jill

Jones Soda Company

JPMorgan Chase & Co.

JV Imaging

Kaiser Permanente

Kali & Kress General Family Dentistry

KBW Financial Staffing and Recruiting

Keynote Speakers

KHI Services, Inc.

KidsFirst

Kimochi Inc.

Kingsbury Club and Spa

KM Lawn, Pet, and House Care

Kmart

Kollsman's

Kopco Graphics Inc.

LA DOTD Federal Credit Union

Label Impressions

Lakeview Concrete ProductsLatino Community Association

Lake Winnipesaukee Golf Club

Leading Authorities Speakers Bureau

Le Groupe Turenne Inc.

LGInternational

LIFE (Let It Flow Enterprises)

Lightning Labels

Lilliput Children's Services

Lilly Pharmaceuticals

Linear Technology Corporation

Littleton Regional Hospital

Logo Tech Inc.

Londonderry Police

LRG Healthcare

LTX Credence

MAG Mortgage Corporation

Majestic Insurance

Manchester High School

Manchester Union Leader

Mantec

Marriott

Martha's Vineyard Insurance Agency

Massachusetts General Hospital

Meals on Wheels of the Salinas Valley

Meijer

Memorial High School

Mentor Graphics Corporation

Merit Resources Inc.

Metropolitan Pipe and Supply

Metso Power

MHF Design Consultants

Microelectrodes

MIG Corporation

Miltope Group Inc.

Mirrus Systems

MIT

Modesto Parent Participation Preschool

Monadnock Community Hospital

Monitor

Multiple Listing Service

Mulvey Professional Association

NAES Power Contractors

Nashua YMCA

National Aeronautics and Space Administration

National Association of Federal Credit Unions

National Australia Bank

National Contract Management Association

National Funeral Directors Association

National Park Service

NBC

NECAPS LLC

Nestle Waters

New Center for Legal Advocacy

New Hampshire Higher Education Assistance Foundation

New Morning Youth & Family Services

Newport Computer Services

Nexage Technologies USA, Inc.

NJ Civil Rights Department

Nonprofit Resource Center

North Cumberland Fire Department

Northern Trust

Northrop Grumman ES

NSTAR

Nuvasive

Office of Senator Judd Gregg

O'Hanlon Center for the Arts

OI Analytical

Oregon College of Oriental Medicine

OrthoBiologics

Osher Marin Jewish Community Center

Owens Corning

Parkinson Association of Northern California

Parkland Medical Center

Parsons

Partners Healthcare

Peg Taylor Center for Adult Day Health Care

People's Place

Periscope

Pfizer Pharmaceuticals LLC

Philips

Pie Head Productions

Pinkerton Academy

Pitney Bowes

Plymouth State University

Pondera Regional Port Authority

Portsmouth Public Library

Portsmouth Regional Hospital

Preble County Council on Aging

Precision Label & Tag Inc.

Premier

Premier Clients

PricewaterhouseCoopers

Prime Revenue

Procedyne Corporation

Project Safeguard

Pulaski Chase Cooperative

Radio-Canada

Randolph Brooks Federal Credit Union

Raytheon Co.

RBI International

Redbox Automated Retail

Reebok

Regan Technologies

RewardsNOW

Rhodia

Richmond District Neighborhood Center

Riverside Medical Clinic Foundation

RMC

Room to Read

Royal Academy of Dance

Royal Computer

Ryder Systems

Rye Fire Department

Safeco Surety

Safe Credit Union

San Francisco Center for the Book

San Group

Sanofi-Aventis

Sapphire Technologies

Schering Plough

School District of Kettle Moraine

Secure Software

Serta Mattress Co., Inc.

Seymour Golf and Country Club

Shasta Women's Refuge

Sheraton

Shure

Sibcy Cline

Sierra Nevada Children's Services

SJE-Rhombus Controls

SleepNet Corporation

Smith & Wesson

Social Security Administration

Software Productivity Center Inc.

Solve IT Inc

Speak Inc.

Sprinkle Home Improvement

Standard Process

Star Alliance Services

Starwood

State of Connecticut Division of Criminal Justice

State of Minnesota

St. John's Preparatory School

Stop & Shop

Strategic Consulting Inc.

Strategic Marketing Partners

Sun Home Health Services

Sun Microsystems

Superior Industries LLC

Suresource

Symantec

Synertel Converged Communications Solutions

Tactical Global Management

Tailored Label Products

Talent Management Consulting

Tandem Professional Employer Services

Tangin, LLC

Target

TargetCast TCM

Tata Consultancy Services

TBA Global

TD Ameritrade

TD Banknorth

Technology Business Research

Terra Firma (HRVP)

Teva Neuroscience

Texas Instruments Inc.

The ABR Group

The Association for Community Living

The Baptist Health Care Leadership Institute

The Common Man

The Higgins Group Realtors

The Staubach Company

The Watsonville Law Center

Thompson Consultants, Inc.

TIAA-CREF

Timberland

TJX Companies

TK-Holdings

Tourism Consultancy

Tower Hill Development and Consulting

Transamerica Retirement Services

Tri-Global Solutions Group Inc.

Trinity Counseling Center

TSE Services

TTI

Tunxis Plantation

Turning Point Recovery Society (1984)

Tyco Electronics

UMASS Memorial Healthcare

Under Armour Performance

United States Environmental Protection Agency

United States Navy

United States Pony Clubs Inc.

United Way Denver

University of New Hampshire

University of Texas

University of Wisconsin Madison

UPS

U.S. Department of Commerce

Valley Oak Children's Services

Valpak of NH Inc

Vanguard

Verizon

Verso Paper

VF Corporation

Vista Bay

VT Milcom

WalkAway USA

Wentworth-Douglass Hospital

Westborough MA Fire Department

Willow Glen Care Center

Wilmington High School

Wilson Research and Development

Wilson Sporting Goods

Wireglass Electric Cooperative

Wisconsin Automobile & Truck
    Dealers Association

WS Packaging Group, Inc.

Yard Restaurant

Yolo Community Care Continuum

Youth in Arts

Zurich North America

THE STUDY CONTINUES

Over the course of the study, we accumulated the world's largest known database of Executive Skills of high-performing individuals in business. The study is now an ongoing study, continuing even through the writing of this book and beyond. Organizations can contact us for information as to how to participate (info@nfiresearch.com). We expect the database to be useful for career planning and advancement.

The High-Performance Executive Skills Tables

Following are the tables comprising the results of the study of high-performing individuals in business. They're broken down by the following categories:

Top Six Industries

Executive Skills by Department: Top 10 Departments

Job Function/Title

Employees vs. Managers vs. Executives

Males vs. Females

Profit vs. Nonprofit

Healthcare: Clinical vs. Nonclinical

Using knowledge of your own Executive Skills strengths, you can scan the entire list to see where your strengths are found in high performers by industry, department, and title. The chapters in this book include only the leading three strengths and weaknesses of high performers. The tables include all 12 skills, sorted first by commonly found strengths and then by commonly found weaknesses.

If you are a manager, you also can use the tables to see the characteristics of high performers in industries or departments like yours. You then can determine if your high performers have the same strengths, and if they do, you will know what characteristic to look for in future hires or promotions.

Top Six Industries

FINANCIAL/INSURANCE/REAL ESTATE
LEADING HIGHS
Metacognition 34%
Goal-Directed Persistence. 34%
Working Memory 32%
Organization 32%
Flexibility 30%
Planning/Prioritization. 28%
Stress Tolerance 23%
Response Inhibition 23%
Emotional Control 19%
Task Initiation 18%
Sustained Attention. 16%
Time Management 12%

LEADING LOWS
Task Initiation 43%
Emotional Control 39%
Organization 34%
Response Inhibition 31%
Stress Tolerance 29%
Time Management 29%
Sustained Attention. 26%
Flexibility 18%
Working Memory 14%
Goal-Directed Persistence. 13%
Metacognition 12%
Planning/Prioritization. 11%

HEALTHCARE/MEDICAL/DENTAL
LEADING HIGHS
Working Memory 37%
Organization 36%
Planning/Prioritization. 35%
Response Inhibition 26%
Flexibility 23%
Metacognition 23%
Task Initiation 22%
Goal-Directed Persistence. 22%
Emotional Control 21%

Time Management 21%
Sustained Attention. 20%
Stress Tolerance 15%

LEADING LOWS
Stress Tolerance 40%
Emotional Control 38%
Task Initiation 38%
Time Management 26%
Response Inhibition 25%
Flexibility 24%
Organization 23%
Sustained Attention. 22%
Goal-Directed Persistence. 21%
Metacognition 19%
Working Memory 13%
Planning/Prioritization. 10%

MANUFACTURING
LEADING HIGHS
Metacognition 36%
Planning/Prioritization. 33%
Organization 31%
Flexibility 31%
Working Memory 29%
Goal-Directed Persistence. 28%
Emotional Control 27%
Response Inhibition 22%
Stress Tolerance 21%
Task Initiation 16%
Sustained Attention. 15%
Time Management 11%

LEADING LOWS
Task Initiation 42%
Time Management 40%
Emotional Control 37%
Organization 37%
Stress Tolerance 31%
Response Inhibition 26%
Sustained Attention. 23%
Working Memory 18%

Goal-Directed Persistence. 16%
Flexibility 15%
Metacognition 9%
Planning/Prioritization. 6%

NONPROFIT/CHARITY
LEADING HIGHS
Working Memory 39%
Organization 33%
Goal-Directed Persistence. 31%
Planning/Prioritization. 30%
Metacognition 29%
Flexibility 27%
Emotional Control 25%
Response Inhibition 23%
Stress Tolerance 20%
Sustained Attention. 18%
Task Initiation 13%
Time Management 11%

LEADING LOWS
Task Initiation 38%
Stress Tolerance 37%
Organization 33%
Sustained Attention. 33%
Emotional Control 32%
Time Management 32%
Response Inhibition 28%
Flexibility 24%
Goal-Directed Persistence. 15%
Metacognition 10%
Planning/Prioritization. 9%
Working Memory 9%

TECHNOLOGY
LEADING HIGHS
Planning/Prioritization. 39%
Working Memory 33%
Organization 32%
Flexibility 31%
Goal-Directed Persistence. 30%

Metacognition 29%
Stress Tolerance 23%
Sustained Attention. 21%
Response Inhibition 19%
Emotional Control 15%
Task Initiation 14%
Time Management 13%

LEADING LOWS
Task Initiation 52%
Emotional Control 38%
Time Management 31%
Organization 30%
Response Inhibition 28%
Stress Tolerance 27%
Sustained Attention. 24%
Metacognition 19%
Flexibility 18%
Goal-Directed Persistence. 13%
Working Memory 12%
Planning/Prioritization. 9%

EDUCATION
SVC./UNIVERSITY/COLLEGE
LEADING HIGHS
Metacognition 31%
Planning/Prioritization. 30%
Organization 30%
Flexibility 29%
Emotional Control 27%
Response Inhibition 26%
Goal-Directed Persistence. 25%
Working Memory 23%
Stress Tolerance 23%
Sustained Attention. 21%
Task Initiation 20%
Time Management 15%

LEADING LOWS
Task Initiation 49%
Time Management 36%
Stress Tolerance 35%

Organization 32%

Response Inhibition 29%

Emotional Control 28%

Sustained Attention................24%

Goal-Directed Persistence...........21%

Flexibility 17%

Working Memory 11%

Metacognition 8%

Planning/Prioritization..............8%

Executive Skills by Department: Top 10 Departments

GENERAL MANAGEMENT
LEADING HIGHS

Metacognition 38%

Planning/Prioritization.............35%

Working Memory 35%

Goal-Directed Persistence...........35%

Organization 31%

Flexibility 29%

Emotional Control 22%

Stress Tolerance 22%

Response Inhibition 22%

Sustained Attention................12%

Time Management 11%

Task Initiation 9%

LEADING LOWS

Task Initiation 49%

Time Management 37%

Emotional Control 36%

Response Inhibition 32%

Sustained Attention................32%

Organization 32%

Stress Tolerance 26%

Flexibility 17%

Working Memory 12%

Metacognition 9%

Planning/Prioritization..............9%

Goal-Directed Persistence............8%

OPERATIONS
LEADING HIGHS

Planning/Prioritization.............36%

Metacognition 32%

Flexibility 31%

Working Memory 30%

Organization 30%

Goal-Directed Persistence...........28%

Stress Tolerance 25%

Response Inhibition 23%

Emotional Control 20%

Sustained Attention................17%

Task Initiation 16%

Time Management 12%

LEADING LOWS

Task Initiation 43%

Emotional Control 38%

Organization 35%

Time Management 33%

Response Inhibition 32%

Stress Tolerance 30%

Sustained Attention................26%

Flexibility 18%

Working Memory 16%

Goal-Directed Persistence...........13%

Metacognition 9%

Planning/Prioritization..............7%

SALES
LEADING HIGHS

Working Memory 42%

Goal-Directed Persistence...........35%

Planning/Prioritization.............30%

Flexibility 30%

Metacognition 30%

Organization 28%

Stress Tolerance 23%

Response Inhibition 22%

Sustained Attention................19%

Emotional Control 18%

Task Initiation 14%

Time Management 10%

LEADING LOWS

Task Initiation 51%

Organization 38%

Emotional Control 38%

Time Management 32%

Response Inhibition 29%

Stress Tolerance 24%

Sustained Attention 24%

Flexibility 18%

Goal-Directed Persistence 13%

Metacognition 11%

Working Memory 11%

Planning/Prioritization 10%

SYSTEMS/IT

LEADING HIGHS

Planning/Prioritization 35%

Metacognition 34%

Working Memory 29%

Flexibility 29%

Response Inhibition 26%

Organization 26%

Stress Tolerance 24%

Emotional Control 23%

Goal-Directed Persistence 23%

Sustained Attention 20%

Task Initiation 16%

Time Management 14%

LEADING LOWS

Task Initiation 44%

Stress Tolerance 38%

Time Management 38%

Emotional Control 32%

Response Inhibition 29%

Organization 26%

Flexibility 24%

Sustained Attention 22%

Goal-Directed Persistence 16%

Working Memory 13%

Metacognition 12%

Planning/Prioritization 5%

**ADVERTISING/MARKETING/
PROMOTION**

LEADING HIGHS

Metacognition 38%

Working Memory 37%

Flexibility 33%

Planning/Prioritization 32%

Organization 31%

Goal-Directed Persistence 30%

Stress Tolerance 22%

Response Inhibition 21%

Task Initiation 16%

Emotional Control 15%

Sustained Attention 12%

Time Management 12%

LEADING LOWS

Task Initiation 47%

Emotional Control 41%

Organization 36%

Response Inhibition 32%

Time Management 29%

Stress Tolerance 27%

Sustained Attention 25%

Flexibility 16%

Working Memory 14%

Metacognition 12%

Goal-Directed Persistence 12%

Planning/Prioritization 8%

CLINICAL

LEADING HIGHS

Organization 39%

Planning/Prioritization 34%

Task Initiation 29%

Working Memory 29%

Response Inhibition 26%

Sustained Attention 23%

Goal-Directed Persistence. 23%

Emotional Control 22%

Time Management 21%

Flexibility 21%

Metacognition 19%

Stress Tolerance 14%

LEADING LOWS

Stress Tolerance 44%

Emotional Control 39%

Goal-Directed Persistence. 29%

Task Initiation 28%

Flexibility 25%

Response Inhibition 24%

Organization 23%

Time Management 23%

Metacognition 21%

Sustained Attention. 19%

Working Memory 16%

Planning/Prioritization. 8%

ADMINISTRATIVE

LEADING HIGHS

Organization 37%

Flexibility 35%

Working Memory 32%

Response Inhibition 26%

Task Initiation 25%

Metacognition 25%

Emotional Control 23%

Planning/Prioritization. 23%

Sustained Attention. 21%

Stress Tolerance 19%

Goal-Directed Persistence. 17%

Time Management 17%

LEADING LOWS

Stress Tolerance 39%

Emotional Control 35%

Task Initiation 32%

Organization 31%

Response Inhibition 31%

Time Management 28%

Sustained Attention. 21%

Goal-Directed Persistence. 21%

Metacognition 20%

Flexibility 17%

Working Memory 13%

Planning/Prioritization. 11%

CUSTOMER SERVICE

LEADING HIGHS

Organization 35%

Flexibility 34%

Planning/Prioritization. 29%

Working Memory 27%

Task Initiation 25%

Time Management 25%

Response Inhibition 23%

Metacognition 23%

Emotional Control 22%

Sustained Attention. 22%

Goal-Directed Persistence. 18%

Stress Tolerance 18%

LEADING LOWS

Stress Tolerance 39%

Task Initiation 34%

Time Management 34%

Emotional Control 31%

Organization 28%

Goal-Directed Persistence. 25%

Response Inhibition 24%

Working Memory 23%

Metacognition 18%

Flexibility 16%

Sustained Attention. 16%

Planning/Prioritization. 14%

FINANCE

LEADING HIGHS

Working Memory 42%

Organization 31%

Flexibility 31%

Planning/Prioritization............29%
Response Inhibition 28%
Emotional Control 26%
Goal-Directed Persistence...........25%
Metacognition 22%
Sustained Attention................20%
Stress Tolerance 20%
Task Initiation 17%
Time Management 9%

LEADING LOWS
Task Initiation 45%
Organization 39%
Emotional Control 39%
Response Inhibition 32%
Time Management 30%
Stress Tolerance 29%
Sustained Attention................22%
Goal-Directed Persistence...........17%
Metacognition 15%
Working Memory 13%
Planning/Prioritization............10%
Flexibility 9%

ACCOUNTING
LEADING HIGHS
Organization 47%
Planning/Prioritization............40%
Working Memory 37%
Goal-Directed Persistence...........27%
Metacognition 23%
Response Inhibition 22%
Sustained Attention................21%
Flexibility 21%
Task Initiation 19%
Emotional Control 16%
Time Management 16%
Stress Tolerance 10%

LEADING LOWS
Stress Tolerance 51%
Emotional Control 37%

Task Initiation 37%
Time Management 37%
Response Inhibition 26%
Flexibility 23%
Sustained Attention................20%
Goal-Directed Persistence...........19%
Metacognition 19%
Organization 14%
Working Memory 11%
Planning/Prioritization.............7%

Job Function/Title

CHAIRMAN/OWNER/PARTNERS
LEADING HIGHS
Metacognition 44%
Working Memory 34%
Flexibility 34%
Response Inhibition 31%
Planning/Prioritization............29%
Goal-Directed Persistence...........27%
Emotional Control 26%
Organization 23%
Sustained Attention................16%
Stress Tolerance 16%
Time Management 13%
Task Initiation 8%

LEADING LOWS
Task Initiation 53%
Sustained Attention................35%
Emotional Control 34%
Organization 29%
Response Inhibition 27%
Time Management 27%
Stress Tolerance 21%
Working Memory 18%
Planning/Prioritization............16%
Flexibility 15%
Metacognition 13%
Goal-Directed Persistence...........11%

CEO

LEADING HIGHS

Goal-Directed Persistence........... 43%
Working Memory 39%
Planning/Prioritization............. 34%
Flexibility 31%
Metacognition 31%
Stress Tolerance 30%
Organization 28%
Emotional Control 17%
Task Initiation 16%
Response Inhibition 14%
Time Management 10%
Sustained Attention................. 9%

LEADING LOWS

Task Initiation 51%
Response Inhibition 40%
Time Management 39%
Emotional Control 37%
Sustained Attention................ 37%
Organization 31%
Stress Tolerance 22%
Flexibility 17%
Working Memory 12%
Metacognition 8%
Goal-Directed Persistence............ 6%
Planning/Prioritization.............. 3%

CFO

LEADING HIGHS

Goal-Directed Persistence........... 45%
Working Memory 41%
Planning/Prioritization............. 39%
Organization 31%
Metacognition 29%
Response Inhibition 24%
Flexibility 24%
Stress Tolerance 20%
Sustained Attention................ 18%
Emotional Control 16%

Task Initiation 12%
Time Management 0%

LEADING LOWS

Time Management 47%
Task Initiation 43%
Emotional Control 39%
Response Inhibition 31%
Organization 31%
Sustained Attention................ 22%
Stress Tolerance 22%
Goal-Directed Persistence........... 18%
Flexibility 18%
Metacognition 12%
Working Memory 8%
Planning/Prioritization.............. 8%

EVP/SVP

LEADING HIGHS

Planning/Prioritization............. 38%
Metacognition 36%
Working Memory 35%
Stress Tolerance 34%
Flexibility 33%
Goal-Directed Persistence........... 27%
Emotional Control 20%
Organization 20%
Response Inhibition 19%
Sustained Attention................ 17%
Task Initiation 13%
Time Management 10%

LEADING LOWS

Task Initiation 49%
Organization 43%
Response Inhibition 41%
Emotional Control 33%
Sustained Attention................ 31%
Time Management 27%
Stress Tolerance 18%
Working Memory 16%
Planning/Prioritization............. 12%

Flexibility 12%
Goal-Directed Persistence. 10%
Metacognition 7%

DIRECTORS
LEADING HIGHS
Working Memory 35%
Goal-Directed Persistence. 35%
Metacognition 34%
Planning/Prioritization. 31%
Flexibility 31%
Organization 25%
Stress Tolerance 25%
Response Inhibition 24%
Emotional Control 24%
Sustained Attention. 15%
Task Initiation 13%
Time Management 8%

LEADING LOWS
Task Initiation 51%
Time Management 39%
Organization 38%
Emotional Control 31%
Sustained Attention. 27%
Stress Tolerance 27%
Response Inhibition 27%
Flexibility 18%
Working Memory 14%
Planning/Prioritization. 9%
Metacognition 9%
Goal-Directed Persistence. 9%

MANAGERS
LEADING HIGHS
Planning/Prioritization. 33%
Organization 32%
Metacognition 32%
Flexibility 32%
Working Memory 30%
Goal-Directed Persistence. 26%
Response Inhibition 25%

Emotional Control 21%
Stress Tolerance 20%
Sustained Attention. 17%
Task Initiation 16%
Time Management 15%

LEADING LOWS
Task Initiation 42%
Emotional Control 38%
Stress Tolerance 33%
Organization 32%
Time Management 31%
Response Inhibition 30%
Sustained Attention. 23%
Flexibility 19%
Working Memory 15%
Goal-Directed Persistence. 14%
Metacognition 13%
Planning/Prioritization. 8%

EMPLOYEES
LEADING HIGHS
Organization 38%
Working Memory 34%
Planning/Prioritization. 28%
Metacognition 27%
Response Inhibition 26%
Flexibility 24%
Task Initiation 23%
Sustained Attention. 22%
Time Management 22%
Emotional Control 20%
Goal-Directed Persistence. 19%
Stress Tolerance 18%

LEADING LOWS
Stress Tolerance 44%
Emotional Control 39%
Task Initiation 36%
Organization 28%
Time Management 24%
Response Inhibition 23%

Flexibility 23%

Goal-Directed Persistence. 22%

Metacognition 18%

Sustained Attention. 17%

Working Memory 15%

Planning/Prioritization. 10%

CONSULTANTS
LEADING HIGHS

Working Memory 41%

Planning/Prioritization. 35%

Organization 31%

Emotional Control 30%

Goal-Directed Persistence. 30%

Sustained Attention. 24%

Response Inhibition 22%

Flexibility 22%

Stress Tolerance 20%

Task Initiation 19%

Metacognition 19%

Time Management 7%

LEADING LOWS

Emotional Control 48%

Task Initiation 37%

Response Inhibition 33%

Stress Tolerance 33%

Time Management 31%

Organization 28%

Flexibility 24%

Sustained Attention. 17%

Working Memory 13%

Planning/Prioritization. 13%

Goal-Directed Persistence. 11%

Metacognition 11%

Employees vs. Managers vs. Executives
EXECUTIVE SKILLS STRENGTHS

	EMPLOYEE	MANAGER	DIRECTOR	EVP/SVP	C TITLE
Response Inhibition					
Working Memory	X		X	X	X
Emotional Control					
Sustained Attention					
Task Initiation					
Planning/Prioritization	X	X		X	X
Organization	X	X			
Time Management					
Goal-Directed Persistence			X		X
Flexibility					
Metacognition		X	X	X	
Stress Tolerance					

EXECUTIVE SKILLS WEAKNESSES

	EMPLOYEE	MANAGER	DIRECTOR	EVP/SVP	C TITLE
Response Inhibition				X	
Working Memory					
Emotional Control	X	X			X
Sustained Attention					
Task Initiation	X	X	X	X	X
Planning/Prioritization					

Organization			X	X	
Time Management			X		X
Goal-Directed Persistence					
Flexibility					
Metacognition					
Stress Tolerance	X	X			

SALES EMPLOYEES VS. SALES MANAGERS VS. SALES EXECUTIVES

Sales Employees

LEADING HIGHS

Working Memory 41%

Metacognition 36%

Flexibility 34%

Planning/Prioritization. 33%

Organization 26%

Goal-Directed Persistence. 26%

Stress Tolerance 24%

Response Inhibition 23%

Emotional Control 16%

Sustained Attention. 16%

Task Initiation 15%

Time Management 14%

LEADING LOWS

Task Initiation 53%

Emotional Control 41%

Organization 40%

Response Inhibition 30%

Time Management 26%

Stress Tolerance 23%

Sustained Attention. 23%

Goal-Directed Persistence. 18%

Flexibility 16%

Metacognition 14%

Working Memory 11%

Planning/Prioritization. 10%

Sales Managers

LEADING HIGHS

Working Memory 41%

Goal-Directed Persistence. 37%

Planning/Prioritization. 34%

Organization 32%

Flexibility 27%

Metacognition 27%

Response Inhibition 21%

Emotional Control 20%

Stress Tolerance 20%

Sustained Attention. 17%

Task Initiation 17%

Time Management 6%

LEADING LOWS

Task Initiation 43%

Emotional Control 40%

Organization 37%

Response Inhibition 35%

Time Management 34%

Stress Tolerance 24%

Sustained Attention. 22%

Flexibility 20%

Metacognition 16%

Goal-Directed Persistence. 11%

Planning/Prioritization. 11%

Working Memory 8%

Sales Executives

LEADING HIGHS

Working Memory 44%

Goal-Directed Persistence. 43%

Flexibility 29%

Metacognition 27%

Stress Tolerance 27%

Sustained Attention. 25%

Planning/Prioritization. 25%

Organization 25%

Response Inhibition 21%

Emotional Control 19%

Task Initiation 11%

Time Management 8%

LEADING LOWS

Task Initiation 60%

Organization 43%

Time Management 37%

Emotional Control 35%

Stress Tolerance 27%

Sustained Attention. 27%

Response Inhibition 25%

Flexibility 17%

Working Memory 12%

Planning/Prioritization. 9%

Goal-Directed Persistence. 8%

Metacognition 4%

**SYSTEMS/IT EMPLOYEES VS.
SYSTEMS/IT MANAGERS VS.
SYSTEMS/IT EXECUTIVES**

Systems/IT Employees
LEADING HIGHS

Metacognition 25%

Working Memory 25%

Planning/Prioritization. 25%

Organization 23%

Response Inhibition 23%

Flexibility 20%

Sustained Attention. 19%

Task Initiation 15%

Time Management 13%

Goal-Directed Persistence. 13%

Emotional Control 11%

Stress Tolerance 8%

LEADING LOWS

Stress Tolerance 38%

Task Initiation 26%

Flexibility 25%

Emotional Control 24%

Time Management 23%

Organization 19%

Goal-Directed Persistence. 18%

Response Inhibition 15%

Metacognition 11%

Sustained Attention. 9%

Working Memory 8%

Planning/Prioritization. 4%

Systems/IT Managers
LEADING HIGHS

Planning/Prioritization. 20%

Response Inhibition 17%

Flexibility 15%

Metacognition 15%

Emotional Control 14%

Organization 13%

Stress Tolerance 12%

Working Memory 9%

Goal-Directed Persistence. 9%

Time Management 8%

Task Initiation 7%

Sustained Attention. 7%

LEADING LOWS

Stress Tolerance 21%

Task Initiation 20%

Time Management 18%

Emotional Control 16%

Response Inhibition 15%

Organization 12%

Working Memory 9%

Sustained Attention. 9%

Flexibility 8%

Goal-Directed Persistence. 7%

Metacognition 5%

Planning/Prioritization. 4%

Systems/IT Executives
LEADING HIGHS

Metacognition 28%

Stress Tolerance 27%

Working Memory 24%

Goal-Directed Persistence. 21%

Flexibility 21%

Planning/Prioritization. 20%

Emotional Control 19%

Organization 17%

Response Inhibition 9%

Sustained Attention. 8%

Task Initiation 8%

Time Management 5%

LEADING LOWS

Task Initiation 39%

Time Management 32%

Sustained Attention. 24%

Response Inhibition 23%

Emotional Control 19%

Organization 17%

Stress Tolerance 16%

Flexibility 16%

Working Memory 8%

Goal-Directed Persistence. 7%

Metacognition 5%

Planning/Prioritization. 3%

**OPERATIONS EMPLOYEES VS.
OPERATIONS MANAGERS VS.
OPERATIONS EXECUTIVES**

Operations Employees
LEADING HIGHS

Organization 29%

Metacognition 28%

Sustained Attention. 26%

Stress Tolerance 24%

Task Initiation 24%

Flexibility 24%

Response Inhibition 24%

Working Memory 24%

Emotional Control 22%

Planning/Prioritization. 22%

Time Management 17%

Goal-Directed Persistence. 14%

LEADING LOWS

Stress Tolerance 41%

Organization 38%

Emotional Control 38%

Task Initiation 31%

Time Management 31%

Flexibility 26%

Response Inhibition 19%

Sustained Attention. 17%

Working Memory 16%

Planning/Prioritization. 9%

Goal-Directed Persistence. 9%

Metacognition 5%

Operations Managers
LEADING HIGHS

Flexibility 37%

Planning/Prioritization. 36%

Organization 31%

Metacognition 31%

Working Memory 30%

Goal-Directed Persistence. 27%

Stress Tolerance 23%

Response Inhibition 21%

Sustained Attention. 19%

Emotional Control 19%

Task Initiation 17%

Time Management 9%

LEADING LOWS

Emotional Control 41%

Task Initiation 40%

Response Inhibition 39%

Organization 35%

Time Management 35%

Stress Tolerance 27%

Sustained Attention. 24%

Flexibility 16%

Working Memory 15%

Goal-Directed Persistence. 14%

Metacognition 11%

Planning/Prioritization. 4%

Operations Executives
LEADING HIGHS
Planning/Prioritization 40%
Goal-Directed Persistence 39%
Metacognition 34%
Stress Tolerance 32%
Flexibility 29%
Working Memory 28%
Response Inhibition 27%
Organization 21%
Emotional Control 20%
Task Initiation 11%
Time Management 10%
Sustained Attention 9%

LEADING LOWS
Task Initiation 61%
Organization 35%
Time Management 35%
Response Inhibition 30%
Sustained Attention 30%
Emotional Control 29%
Stress Tolerance 23%
Working Memory 20%
Flexibility 12%
Goal-Directed Persistence 10%
Planning/Prioritization 9%
Metacognition 6%

ADMINISTRATIVE EMPLOYEES VS. ADMINISTRATIVE MANAGERS VS. ADMINISTRATIVE EXECUTIVES
Administrative Employees
LEADING HIGHS
Organization 62%
Working Memory 30%
Response Inhibition 27%
Task Initiation 27%
Flexibility 27%
Emotional Control 24%
Sustained Attention 24%
Time Management 22%

Metacognition 22%
Planning/Prioritization 14%
Stress Tolerance 14%
Goal-Directed Persistence 8%

LEADING LOWS
Stress Tolerance 62%
Emotional Control 43%
Metacognition 32%
Response Inhibition 30%
Goal-Directed Persistence 27%
Task Initiation 24%
Time Management 22%
Organization 16%
Working Memory 16%
Flexibility 11%
Planning/Prioritization 11%
Sustained Attention 8%

Administrative Managers
LEADING HIGHS
Organization 42%
Flexibility 35%
Working Memory 29%
Task Initiation 29%
Sustained Attention 26%
Time Management 26%
Stress Tolerance 26%
Emotional Control 23%
Response Inhibition 19%
Metacognition 19%
Planning/Prioritization 16%
Goal-Directed Persistence 13%

LEADING LOWS
Organization 35%
Stress Tolerance 32%
Response Inhibition 32%
Goal-Directed Persistence 32%
Emotional Control 29%
Working Memory 26%
Flexibility 23%
Metacognition 23%

Task Initiation 19%
Time Management 16%
Planning/Prioritization. 16%
Sustained Attention. 13%

Administrative Executives
LEADING HIGHS
Flexibility 45%
Working Memory 43%
Planning/Prioritization. 33%
Response Inhibition 30%
Metacognition 28%
Goal-Directed Persistence. 25%
Sustained Attention. 23%
Emotional Control 18%
Stress Tolerance 18%
Task Initiation 15%
Organization 13%
Time Management 13%

LEADING LOWS
Task Initiation 50%
Time Management 40%
Sustained Attention. 35%
Organization 35%
Emotional Control 30%
Response Inhibition 28%
Stress Tolerance 23%
Flexibility 20%
Metacognition 15%
Goal-Directed Persistence. 13%
Planning/Prioritization. 8%
Working Memory 5%

CUSTOMER SERVICE EMPLOYEES VS. CUSTOMER SERVICE MANAGERS

Customer Service Employees
LEADING HIGHS
Organization 38%
Working Memory 30%
Time Management 30%

Task Initiation 28%
Flexibility 28%
Sustained Attention. 27%
Planning/Prioritization. 23%
Metacognition 23%
Response Inhibition 22%
Emotional Control 22%
Goal-Directed Persistence. 15%
Stress Tolerance 15%

LEADING LOWS
Stress Tolerance 53%
Emotional Control 37%
Organization 27%
Goal-Directed Persistence. 27%
Time Management 25%
Task Initiation 22%
Response Inhibition 22%
Working Memory 20%
Flexibility 20%
Metacognition 20%
Planning/Prioritization. 18%
Sustained Attention. 10%

Customer Service Managers
LEADING HIGHS
Planning/Prioritization. 47%
Flexibility 38%
Response Inhibition 32%
Working Memory 26%
Organization 26%
Metacognition 26%
Emotional Control 24%
Time Management 24%
Sustained Attention. 21%
Task Initiation 15%
Stress Tolerance 12%
Goal-Directed Persistence. 9%

LEADING LOWS
Task Initiation 44%
Organization 32%

Stress Tolerance 32%

Working Memory 29%

Time Management 29%

Emotional Control 26%

Sustained Attention 26%

Response Inhibition 24%

Goal-Directed Persistence 21%

Metacognition 18%

Flexibility 12%

Planning/Prioritization 6%

Males vs. Females

MALES

LEADING HIGHS

Metacognition 35%

Planning/Prioritization 33%

Working Memory 31%

Goal-Directed Persistence 31%

Flexibility 31%

Organization 26%

Stress Tolerance 25%

Emotional Control 24%

Response Inhibition 24%

Sustained Attention 15%

Task Initiation 14%

Time Management 12%

LEADING LOWS

Task Initiation 46%

Organization 38%

Emotional Control 34%

Time Management 33%

Response Inhibition 32%

Stress Tolerance 26%

Sustained Attention 25%

Flexibility 17%

Working Memory 16%

Goal-Directed Persistence 12%

Metacognition 12%

Planning/Prioritization 9%

FEMALES

LEADING HIGHS

Organization 38%

Working Memory 37%

Planning/Prioritization 31%

Flexibility 28%

Metacognition 27%

Goal-Directed Persistence 24%

Response Inhibition 22%

Task Initiation 20%

Sustained Attention 20%

Emotional Control 18%

Stress Tolerance 17%

Time Management 17%

LEADING LOWS

Emotional Control 41%

Stress Tolerance 41%

Task Initiation 39%

Time Management 29%

Response Inhibition 27%

Organization 26%

Sustained Attention 23%

Flexibility 21%

Goal-Directed Persistence 19%

Metacognition 14%

Working Memory 12%

Planning/Prioritization 9%

Profit vs. Nonprofit

PROFIT

LEADING HIGHS

Working Memory 33%

Planning/Prioritization 32%

Organization 32%

Metacognition 31%

Flexibility 29%

Goal-Directed Persistence 27%

Response Inhibition 24%

Stress Tolerance 21%

Emotional Control 21%

Sustained Attention. 18%

Task Initiation 17%

Time Management 15%

LEADING LOWS

Task Initiation 43%

Emotional Control 37%

Stress Tolerance 33%

Organization 32%

Time Management 32%

Response Inhibition 29%

Sustained Attention. 23%

Flexibility 19%

Goal-Directed Persistence. 15%

Working Memory 15%

Metacognition 13%

Planning/Prioritization. 9%

NONPROFIT

LEADING HIGHS

Working Memory 39%

Organization 33%

Goal-Directed Persistence. 31%

Planning/Prioritization. 31%

Metacognition 29%

Flexibility 28%

Emotional Control 25%

Response Inhibition 23%

Stress Tolerance 20%

Sustained Attention. 18%

Task Initiation 12%

Time Management 10%

LEADING LOWS

Task Initiation 39%

Stress Tolerance 37%

Organization 33%

Sustained Attention. 33%

Emotional Control 32%

Time Management 32%

Response Inhibition 28%

Flexibility 23%

Goal-Directed Persistence. 15%

Metacognition 10%

Planning/Prioritization. 9%

Working Memory 9%

Profit vs. Nonprofit
(Excluding CEOs)
PROFIT

LEADING HIGHS

Working Memory 31%

Planning/Prioritization. 30%

Organization 30%

Metacognition 30%

Flexibility 28%

Goal-Directed Persistence. 25%

Response Inhibition 23%

Emotional Control 20%

Stress Tolerance 20%

Sustained Attention. 17%

Task Initiation 17%

Time Management 14%

LEADING LOWS

Task Initiation 41%

Emotional Control 35%

Stress Tolerance 32%

Organization 31%

Time Management 30%

Response Inhibition 27%

Sustained Attention. 21%

Flexibility 18%

Goal-Directed Persistence. 15%

Working Memory 14%

Metacognition 13%

Planning/Prioritization. 9%

NONPROFIT

LEADING HIGHS

Working Memory 32%

Organization 30%

Planning/Prioritization............. 26%

Goal-Directed Persistence........... 25%

Flexibility 23%

Metacognition 22%

Emotional Control 22%

Response Inhibition 19%

Sustained Attention................ 17%

Stress Tolerance 15%

Task Initiation 12%

Time Management 8%

LEADING LOWS

Stress Tolerance 33%

Task Initiation 29%

Organization 28%

Emotional Control 28%

Time Management 26%

Sustained Attention................ 25%

Flexibility 21%

Response Inhibition 21%

Goal-Directed Persistence........... 13%

Metacognition 10%

Planning/Prioritization............. 9%

Working Memory 7%

Healthcare: Clinical vs. Nonclinical

HEALTHCARE—CLINICAL DEPARTMENTS—124 SURVEYS

LEADING HIGHS

Organization 38%

Planning/Prioritization............. 35%

Task Initiation 30%

Working Memory 27%

Response Inhibition 27%

Time Management 24%

Sustained Attention................ 23%

Goal-Directed Persistence........... 23%

Flexibility 21%

Emotional Control 19%

Metacognition 18%

Stress Tolerance 16%

LEADING LOWS

Stress Tolerance 44%

Emotional Control 43%

Goal-Directed Persistence........... 29%

Task Initiation 27%

Response Inhibition 26%

Flexibility 23%

Organization 22%

Time Management 22%

Metacognition 22%

Sustained Attention................ 18%

Working Memory 17%

Planning/Prioritization............. 9%

HEALTHCARE—NONCLINICAL DEPARTMENTS—154 SURVEYS

LEADING HIGHS

Working Memory 44%

Planning/Prioritization............. 36%

Organization 33%

Metacognition 27%

Response Inhibition 26%

Flexibility 25%

Emotional Control 23%

Goal-Directed Persistence........... 22%

Sustained Attention................ 18%

Task Initiation 16%

Stress Tolerance 16%

Time Management 14%

LEADING LOWS

Task Initiation 48%

Stress Tolerance 36%

Emotional Control 35%

Time Management 31%

Organization 27%

Flexibility 26%

Sustained Attention. . . . . 25%   Goal-Directed Persistence. 12%

Response Inhibition . . . . 24%   Working Memory 10%

Metacognition . . . . 16%   Planning/Prioritization. 10%

About NFI Research

Every two weeks, NFI Research sends surveys via e-mail to 2,000 executives and managers in 50 countries. The surveys are short, and results are anonymous. These surveys have been conducted every two weeks for the past 10 years.

When the questions list potential answers, NFI Research asks respondents in the panel to check all answers that apply, thereby providing a majority consensus in results. The surveys do not necessarily match intensity of feeling about any given subject, but rather what the majority of respondents agrees and disagrees on. NFI Research repeats some surveys over the years, so that benchmarking is possible and changes in attitude are identified. NFI does not share the e-mail addresses or any personal information about any of its members. There is no charge for membership, and the members all receive the survey results every other week for free. Response rates are typically at least 10 percent or higher. NFI Research survey results are routinely reported in newspapers, magazines, newsletters, and blogs around the world.

Survey participants fall into one of two categories: senior executive (chief executive officer, chairman, president, chief operating officer, chief financial officer, chief information officer, executive vice president, senior vice president, general manager, etc.) or manager (assistant vice president, director, manager, supervisor, etc.). Respondents are usually about half senior executives and half managers. Some percentages do not equal 100 percent due to rounding. All research in the book, unless otherwise stated, is primary research conducted by NFI Research.

Respondents also identify themselves by company size, based on the total number of employees, and the results generally are a fairly even split among the groups. Some of those differences, as well as those between senior executives and managers, are used in the book when there are differences worth noting. Company sizes are based on the number of employees, with small having 1 to 499 employees, medium 500 to 9,999, and large with 10,000 or more employees.

A small sampling of the more than 1,000 companies for which members work are IBM, Hewlett-Packard, Borders, Morgan Stanley, Microsoft, Merck, Motorola, Freddie Mac, Progressive, MasterCard, SAP, Oracle, Marriott International, Mercer, American Cancer Society, Allstate, Heineken, Western Energy Institute, Walmart, Wells Fargo, Air Canada, Allied Waste Industries, American Association of Advertising Agencies, American Cancer Society, American Express, 3M Company, AT&T, Bank of America, Bell Canada, Best Buy, California Credit Union League, Bristol-Meyers Squibb Company, Canon, and Procter & Gamble.

You may obtain further information at www.nfiresearch.com, where, if you are a senior executive or manager, you may apply for free membership. You may also contact coauthor Chuck Martin directly at chuck@nfiresearch.com and follow him on Twitter @chuckmartin1.

INTRODUCTION

1. Author Jim Collins popularized this concept in the book *Good to Great*.
2. Details of how the study was conducted are included in a later chapter.
3. The Executive Skills Survey has been used in the marketplace for several years to determine the Executive Skills strengths and weaknesses of people in business.

CHAPTER 1

1. Based on survey conducted by NFI Research.

CHAPTER 2

1. Hart, T., & Jacobs, H. E. (1993). Rehabilitation and management of behavioral disturbances following frontal lobe injury. *Journal of Head Trauma Rehabilitation, 8*, 1–12.
2. Kolb, B., & Wishaw, Q. (1990). *Fundamentals of human neuropsychology* (3rd ed.). New York: W.H. Freeman.
3. Pliszka, S. R. (2002). Neuroimaging and ADHD: Recent progress. *The ADHD Report, 10*(3), 1–6.
4. Hart, T., & Jacobs, H. E. (1993). Rehabilitation and management of behavioral disturbances following frontal lobe injury. *Journal of Head Trauma Rehabilitation, 8*, 2–3.
5. Goldberg, E. (2001). *The executive brain*. Oxford, UK: Oxford University Press.

CHAPTER 3

1. Based on author Chuck Martin's interview of Geri Rhoades, vice president of organizational development at Cafco.
2. Based on author Chuck Martin's interview of Lori McLeese, chief people officer of Room to Read.
3. Based on author Chuck Martin's interview of Tom Ortner, executive director of Willow Glen Care Center.
4. Based on author Chuck Martin's interview with Michele Frisby, director of public information at the International City/County Management Association.
5. Based on author Chuck Martin's interview with Nancy Benullo, footwear product director in the Ryka division of American Sporting Goods.

6. Based on author Chuck Martin's interview with Sandra Lambert of Tri-Global Solutions.

7. Based on author Chuck Martin's interview with Howard Elton, technical manager at Rhodia.

8. Based on author Chuck Martin's interview with Don Boatright, president of Higher-I.T. Company.

9. Based on author Chuck Martin's interview with Pamela Davis, president and CEO of Alliance Member Services.

10. Based on author Chuck Martin's interview with Nancy Reinhardt of the New Jersey Civil Rights Department.

11. Based on author Chuck Martin's interviews with James Bartlett, executive director of the North Dakota Home School Association, and Brooke Frost, executive director of Big Brothers Big Sisters of Central California.

12. Based on author Chuck Martin's interview with Laina Aylward, administrative assistant and director of homeowner services at the Bridges Resort and Tennis Club.

13. Based on author Chuck Martin's interview with Florence Bishop, executive director of Trinity Counseling Center.

14. Based on author Chuck Martin's interview with Mark Katz, chief information officer at Esselte.

15. Based on author Chuck Martin's interview with George Brennan, executive vice president of sales and marketing at Interstate Hotels and Resorts.

16. Based on author Chuck Martin's interview with Greg D. Johnson, president of Euro RSCG Edge.

17. Based on author Chuck Martin's interview with David A. Miller, finance vice president at SUN Home Health Services.

18. Based on author Chuck Martin's interview with Sue Miller, vice president of knowledge development at the Wisconsin Automobile and Truck Dealers Association.

19. Based on author Chuck Martin's interview with Darlene Marstaller of the human resources department at Verso Paper.

20. Based on author Chuck Martin's interview with Dawn Harris, executive vice president and chief operating officer of Campus Federal Credit Union.

21. Based on author Chuck Martin's interview with Patrick F. Murphy, senior vice president of implementation service at ING.

22. Based on author Chuck Martin's interview with Chris Harper, dean of academic affairs at Pinkerton Academy.

23. Based on author Chuck Martin's interview with Jim Doyle, partner and electronics industry solutions leader for the Americas at IBM Global Business Services.

24. Based on author Chuck Martin's interview with Megan Wilkinson, executive director of the O'Hanlon Center for the Arts.

25. Based on author Chuck Martin's interview with Jeri Shumate, executive director of 211info.

CHAPTER 4

1. CEOs were excluded from both for-profits and nonprofits since there was a disproportionate number of CEOs in the nonprofits group.

2. Ninety-one percent of high performers in nonprofits are not weak in Working Memory.

CHAPTER 5

1. Planning/Prioritization was almost a tie with Flexibility as one of the leading three strengths.

2. Emotional Control is a strength in only about one-sixth of high performers in marketing.

3. The same percentage of high performers possesses these two skills.

4. Based on results of a survey of senior executives and managers conducted by NFI Research.

5. Working Memory is the fourth most commonly found strength in high performers in customer service.

6. Based on author Chuck Martin's interview with John Nadeau, president of Chest PT Services, a participant in the study.

CHAPTER 6

1. Thirty-eight percent of those with a chief title are strong in Planning/Prioritization.

2. Forty-seven percent of those with C titles are weak in Time Management, eight times more than those who are strong in it.

3. More than 40 percent of chiefs are weak in Emotional Control.

4. Ninety-three percent of executive and senior vice presidents are not weak in Metacognition, and 36 percent count it as an Executive Skills strength.

5. Thirty-five percent of high-performing directors are strong in Working Memory or Goal-Directed Persistence. Thirty-four percent are strong in Metacognition.

6. Fifty-one percent of directors are weak in Task Initiation, 39 percent are weak in Time Management, and 38 percent are weak in Organization.

CHAPTER 7

1. Based on author Chuck Martin's interview with Pamela E. Davis, president and chief executive officer of AMS.

2. Based on author Chuck Martin's interview with Peggy Entrekin, executive director of United States Pony Clubs, Inc.

3. Based on author Chuck Martin's interview with Maggie John, executive director of Shasta Women's Refuge.

4. The study, "Observable Cognitive Function in the Purchasing Process: A Study of Quickly Identifying Impulse Buying Behaviors in Consumers," was conducted by a 50-person research team at the Whittemore School of Business and Economics at the University of New Hampshire, led by Chuck Martin.

5. The study, "Observable Cognitive Function in the Purchasing Process of TVs, High-End Electronics: A Study of Identifying Impulse Buying Behaviors in Consumers," was conducted by a 41-person research team at the Whittemore School of Business and Economics at the University of New Hampshire, led by Chuck Martin.

6. We created a list of questions for each skill that would be used to validate the observations, based on a Likert scale of one to five (do not agree to highly agree). The questions were designed to measure certain cognitive capabilities in an individual, specifically whether

the person was high or low in the Executive Skills of Response Inhibition and/or Flexibility.

7. In the first study, after 55 unique observations from more than 40 retail locations, 52 of the 55 observations were shown to be correct based on answers to the high/low cognitive function questions, a validation rate of 95 percent. The research teams visited various retail outlets, retail stores, grocery stores, gas stations, quick-serve locations, and convenience stores in the New Hampshire seacoast area, in the towns of Dover, Durham, Lee, and Portsmouth. Locations included Wal-Mart, Best Buy, Nordstrom, and the Fox Run Mall.

8. An *action* involved either body language or physical reactions that could be related to a point of purchase and was clearly observable. For example, one researcher observed a consumer who appeared to be interested in televisions. The teams noticed that the customer quickly became agitated when told the model in which he was interested was not in stock. From this observation, the researcher perceived the customer to be low in Flexibility, which was validated based on answers to the questions after the consumer left the store.

9. The 41 researchers were divided into six teams. Like in the first study, the accuracy of the observations was determined by a series of questions answered by the subjects that identified specific high and low Executive Skills in the individuals.

10. To conduct the observations, the researchers watched consumers throughout the purchasing process, from the time they entered the store to when a purchase was or was not made. Based on a consumer's actions, the research teams perceived whether the consumer was high or low in either of the two Executive Skills.

11. To validate their observations, the researchers asked the consumer specific questions pertaining to the Executive Skill after the shopper left the store. From their answers, it could be determined whether the observation was validated. Of 76 observations, 74 were validated by answers to the questions after the shoppers left the stores. This was a validation rate of 97 percent, meaning the identification of a specific Executive Skill, based on the behaviors the researchers observed, was shown to be correct 97 percent of the time, based on answers to the questions.

12. For example, in the case of a shopper high in Flexibility, the person can be recognized by certain actions, such as walking around looking at all different TV sizes and makes. He does not look partial to a particular brand. A sales representative approaches the man and offers a few suggestions. The rep then asks if the man has something in mind, and the man replies, "Pretty good quality, pretty good price." After that, the salesperson tells the man to buy a certain TV and the man agrees. The buyer does not have a particular brand preference and is open to all forms of suggestions. These characteristics are consistent in consumers high in Flexibility.

13. They are likely to come into the store with a particular item in mind but buy a different one recommended by a salesperson. In many cases in the second study, a customer would look at several televisions, ask the salesperson what he or she recommended, and purchase that model. In one case, a woman came into a store with a piece of paper noting the television she desired, which she changed after the salesperson made a suggestion.

14. In the TV and high-end electronics study, buyers consistently changed their minds about a television purchase multiple times in the course of the purchase cycle. They would look at a variety of models from various makers and purchase a different brand just because one they originally wanted was not in stock. These buyers are very willing to buy a substitute product.

15. They will leave a store with product information, but not the product. They are hesitant to make a purchase even after deciding on a specific TV, for example, and will wait to purchase it. They can have a product in their hand the entire time and still not ultimately purchase it. They tend to have strong product preference and will go to another store if that store does not have the exact product they want.

16. They will pick up and buy more items on the way out. They may go into the store with the intent to purchase a product (television) and then purchase it and pick up other goods when cashing out or even buy a sound system rather than the intended TV because it is on sale. They tend to look at sales items and spend more than originally planned.

CHAPTER 8

1. In customer service, study participants were mostly at the employee and manager level, so we excluded executives from the results.

2. The eight classes comprised junior and senior marketing majors at the Whittemore School of Business and Economics at the University of New Hampshire. Each person completed the Executive Skills profile, the same questionnaire used in the high-performers study for team placements. Class sizes ranged from 20 to 40 students each.

CHAPTER 9

1. When we segment Executive Skills strengths by departments, we use the 12 departments where the largest number of high performers in our study work.

2. Since there were a different number of high performers possessing each of the 12 Executive Skills, we weighted the numbers based on the number of respondents with each skill in each title or department.

APPENDIX A

1. To test the reliability of the Executive Skills questionnaire a test/retest study was completed among 30 individuals. All study participants completed the 60-item questionnaire with five-point rating scales on each of the five statements corresponding to the 12 Executive Skills. Scores were recorded and profiles were computed for each of the participants. In a second phase, the same participants completed the questionnaire again and their scores were recorded and compared to their first responses. The instrument demonstrated remarkable test/retest reliability with an average Cronbach's alpha statistic of .92 across all Executive Skills. This level of reliability is well above the accepted standards for attitudinal survey instruments, and demonstrates that individuals are stable in their evaluation of which Executive Skill profile statements are the most personally relevant.